Praise for *Confessions of an Adoptive Parent*

As an adoptee, I'm always a little leery of books about adoption because I don't know what angle they will take. Will they make adoptees sound like problem children? Will they come across bleak or disparaging? But after reading this book, I feel refreshed and encouraged. It's real and honest but filled with hope. I recommend it to any foster or adoptive parent (as well as adoptees!).

Tony Wolf
author of *Serve One*

As the father of three biological children, I never knew the challenges or the amazingness of being an adoptive or foster parent. In *Confessions of an Adoptive Parent*, Mike takes you on a journey filled with hope and accurately captures the beauty of being an adoptive parent. You will laugh, you will cry, and you will be filled with a sense of deep hope. It's a must-read for anyone on this journey, or considering it!

Jackie Bledsoe
speaker and author of *The 7 Rings of Marriage*

With rare transparency, Mike Berry reveals the raw realities of parenting adopted and foster kids. What a gift to adoptive parents to find validation and know they are not alone! This is a must-read for every adoptive and foster parent who needs edification and encouragement. Highly recommended.

Sherrie Eldridge
author of *20 Things Adopted Kids Wish Their Adoptive Parents Knew*

As Mike says, "this journey is not meant to be lived alone." Thanks to this book, it doesn't have to be. *Confessions of an Adoptive Parent* provides guidance and desperately needed comfort, healing, and hope to parents who are struggling. I am grateful to reap the wisdom of Mike's authentic testimony; his words are laced with grace, conviction, and reassurance. Mike's transparency weaves together stories of pain that has been lifted by abundant purpose, and through his encouraging book, we come to recognize our real need for Jesus in our struggles and the intense beauty found in the mess.

lake
tiful

Doing good is simple and significant, but that does not mean it's easy. Mike reminds us that caring for vulnerable kids is in fact hard. However, he gives us the practical tools we need to find comfort and success as we struggle to love and bring hope to those who are in need of a healthy family.

Chris Marlow
founder and CEO of Help One Now
author of *Doing Good Is Simple*

In *Confessions of an Adoptive Parent*, Mike Berry speaks right into that place seldom spoken of outside support groups huddled in church basements or conferences for foster and adoptive parents. His words are helpful, his words are true, and his words help us see our lives and work as parents in the proper perspective. Even though the road is long and sometimes grueling, Mike continually leads us back to the hope we have not only for our children's futures, but for all of us in Christ.

Amanda Bacon
cocreator of *TheMasterpieceMom.com*

This book contains the words adoptive parents long for, plus many of the statements we are afraid to voice ourselves. *Confessions of an Adoptive Parent* is validating, reassuring, encouraging, and clearly written by someone who has slogged through the trenches of adoption and is still standing there, hip-deep, reaching out to help the stumbling. Mike Berry knows grief and grit, and he speaks our language.

Shannon Guerra
author of *Upside Down:*
Understanding and Supporting Attachment in Adoptive Families

Mike Berry shares his journey as a foster and adoptive parent with unmatched candor, humor, and insight. From uncertainty to optimism, reality to discouragement, and finally to a deep reservoir of hope, he walks parents through his story, giving us courage for our own. *Confessions of an Adoptive Parent* is a fresh reminder to parents in all phases of the foster and adoptive journey that we are not alone. There is a community ready to surround us and a loving God who will never leave us.

Lisa Qualls
writer/speaker/encourager at *OneThankfulMom.com*

I greatly value Mike Berry's frank and winsome voice. Mike is both insightful and funny, gutsy and compassionate, and he consistently brings together big-picture perspective with nitty-gritty practicality. I imagine most all of us wish we could have a friend like Mike in our corner, especially amid difficult foster and adoption journeys. Through this book, we all can.

Jedd Medefind
president, Christian Alliance for Orphans
author of *Becoming Home*

As an adoptive dad of three, a nonprofit adoptions attorney, and founder of a national conference for foster and adoptive parents, by far the most common thing I hear from other foster/adoptive parents is "We feel so alone" or "We feel like nobody 'gets' us." If that's you, this book is for you! The word "Confessions" in this title is perfect—Mike Berry is not just writing words on a page, he's telling his story. And I'll bet you'll find parts of it are your story too. Mike's been where you are…in fact, he is still there right along with you! If you need to be encouraged, if you need to laugh, or if you need a reminder that your insane, jacked-up life as a foster/adoptive parent isn't so strange after all, read this book. You can thank me later.

Andrew Schneidler
nonprofit adoptions attorney
cofounder of the Refresh Conference

I love this book! In *Confessions of an Adoptive Parent*, Mike Berry has written a wonderful resource for adoptive and foster parents who are in the trenches of caring for vulnerable children or considering the journey. You will truly feel understood. Mike doesn't shy away from the challenges of the journey, but offers hope and practical strategies for parents on every page.

Jenn Ranter
founder and director of Replanted Ministry
managing director, Humanitarian Disaster Institute, Wheaton College

This book is a phenomenal resource for any adoptive or foster parent looking for help and hope along their journey. If you need encouragement, guidance, and assurance that you are not alone in your circumstances, you need to buy this book.

Jason Jones
author of *Limping but Blessed: Wrestling with God After the Death of a Child*

CONFESSIONS

of an

Adoptive Parent

MIKE
BERRY

HARVEST HOUSE PUBLISHERS
EUGENE, OREGON

Unless otherwise indicated, all Scripture quotations are taken from the Holy Bible, New International Version®, NIV®. Copyright © 1973, 1978, 1984, 2011 by Biblica, Inc.® Used by permission. All rights reserved worldwide.

Verses marked NLT are taken from the *Holy Bible*, New Living Translation, copyright ©1996, 2004, 2007, 2013 by Tyndale House Foundation. Used by permission of Tyndale House Publishers, Inc., Carol Stream, Illinois 60188. All rights reserved.

Cover design by Bryce Williamson

Cover photos © paci77, Hibrida13 / iStock

Interior design by Janelle Coury

Published in association with Hartline Literary Agency, LLC, of 123 Queenston Drive, Pittsburgh, PA 15235.

CONFESSIONS OF AN ADOPTIVE PARENT

Copyright © 2017 Mike Berry
Published by Harvest House Publishers
Eugene, Oregon 97408
www.harvesthousepublishers.com

ISBN 978-0-7369-7083-9 (pbk.)
ISBN 978-0-7369-7084-6 (eBook)

Library of Congress Cataloging-in-Publication Data

Names: Berry, Mike (Parenting blogger), author.
Title: Confessions of an adoptive parent : hope and help from the trenches of foster care and adoption / Mike Berry.
Description: Eugene, Oregon : Harvest House Publishers, 2018.
Identifiers: LCCN 2017016830 (print) | LCCN 2017040724 (ebook) | ISBN 9780736970846 (ebook) | ISBN 9780736970839 (paperback)
Subjects: LCSH: Foster parents. | Adoptive parents. | Parenting. | BISAC: RELIGION / Christian Life / Family.
Classification: LCC HQ759.7 (ebook) | LCC HQ759.7 .B47 2018 (print) | DDC 306.874—dc23
LC record available at https://lccn.loc.gov/2017016830

Printed in the United States of America

17 18 19 20 21 22 23 24 25 / VP-JC / 10 9 8 7 6 5 4 3 2 1

To Kristin—
your belief in me is overwhelming.
You're a way better human being than I'll ever be.
Thank you for suggesting we go on this journey in the first place.
Forever yours.

To Rachel, Krystal, Noelle, Jaala, Andre,
Elisha, Jacob, and Samuel—
you're the reason this book exists.
Thank you for making my heart warm every day.
I love you more than anything.

Contents

 Introduction

I stand in the back of a church auditorium in western Washington State packed with nearly 2000 foster and adoptive parents. We've come from all walks of life and all parts of the United States. Some have even gathered from Mexico, Canada, Europe, and Australia. We're excited to be together and eager to learn how to be the best parents we can be. But we also wear scars from a journey that has nearly taken the life out of us. What began with passion, calling, and a drive to be light in hurting children's lives has proven to be exhausting and defeating on multiple levels. I understand these parents' scars. I have some too.

All of us in this auditorium have one thing in common—we love our kids. Deeply, in fact. We stand here together because we've been called to this great journey. We were chosen to love and lead children from difficult places. We rose to the challenge and jumped off. But soon we discovered how much we didn't know or weren't prepared for. We also quickly discovered how much our decision to adopt has confused other people. They ask us, "Why would you bring children who aren't yours into your home?" But those of us in this room know. And we understand each other's longings, hopes, dreams, fears, and anxieties.

The lights go dark, and everyone takes their seat. Suddenly the enormous video screen center stage illuminates with the image of a person walking onto a film set. He sits down, looks into the camera and says the words, "You are not alone," with compassion in his voice. He is followed by a woman who repeats the same sentence. One by one, more people appear on screen, saying...

- "You are not alone if you have days where you think, 'Did I make the right choice in adopting my child?'"
- "You are not alone if, as a foster parent, you've laid awake at night, praying for a child who no longer lives with you."
- "You are not alone if you feel utterly incapable of meeting the needs of the children in your care."
- "You are not alone if the journey you've taken as a parent has caused you to lose some friends."
- "You are not alone if your life has become an alphabet soup of things like PTSD, ADHD, FASD, ARND, and so on."
- "You are not alone if you swear more now than you did when you were in high school."
- "You are not alone if the mountain of paperwork your caseworker has you fill out has caused you to develop an involuntary twitch."

You may laugh at those last few, but if you're a foster or adoptive parent, you totally understand what I'm talking about. In fact…you are not alone!

As each person appears and speaks, my wife and I feel peace wash over us like warm water. We inhale and slowly exhale. I feel her hand grab hold of mine. We interlock fingers and hold on tight to each other. It's been a rough few months. We love our children, and we want to be the best parents we can be, but we're tired. We've looked at each other with the same thought: "I don't know if I can keep going." We've been invited to this conference as speakers, but we're so in need of rest we can barely keep our eyes open. Between attending therapy appointments, figuring out which medications work with our son's disorder, getting the elementary school on the same page with us, and parenting through trauma (our children's and our own), we have moments when we feel like quitting.

Like most who begin this journey, we started with such hope, such passion. Nothing was going to stop us. We were ready to love and care for the most difficult child placed in our care. We looked at the mountain standing before us and, with a drive that could rival an NFL running back, we charged ahead. We could hurdle any obstacle standing in our way, right? We could overcome any trial, challenge, battle, or barrier, right? We knew this path would include obstacles, but we were confident we could overcome them. All we needed to do was love the children who came into our home. That would be enough to lead them through whatever trauma they had endured, right?

> We soon discovered just how unprepared for this journey we really were.

How naive we were! How clueless! We soon discovered just how unprepared for this journey we really were. For all our passion, we had no direction. We knew in our hearts that we were called to love children from vulnerable places, but we had no idea just how difficult this task would be at times. There was no manual, no user's guide, no expert sitting down with us to explain separation anxiety, attachment issues, the effects of prenatal drug exposure, or how any of this would manifest itself in our daily lives.

But there, like a beacon of light for a ship in danger of being dashed on the jagged rocks of the shoreline, is a message so simple, yet so profound...You are not alone.

We walked into that conference empty, but we left changed, renewed, rejuvenated, and overflowing with hope. What happened in two short days transformed us and gave us new perspective on the foster and adoptive journey.

I share that story for one reason. I know where you are. I see you. In fact, I *am* you. Maybe you are feeling empty. Perhaps the journey hasn't been what you thought it would be. You love your kids—no question about that—but you're drained. You feel isolated and lonely more days than not. My hope is that as you read this book, you will be transformed and filled with hope, just as we were at that conference.

In this book, we're going to explore this profound message. I'm going to share true hope with you and where I believe it's found. I'm going to relate honest stories and moments from my own life, when our journey was in peril and looked like a pile of ashes. I'll tell the story of how a loving God reached down and pulled me out through the most unlikely circumstances. I'll describe the hope Kristin and I have found even in the biggest storms. Whether you're just beginning this journey or you've been on it for a while, you can find the same hope I have. My hope and prayer is that by the time you close this book, you will realize two things:

You are not alone!
There is hope!

Are you ready? Let's get going. This journey is hard—there's no doubt about it. It can take the life out of you and make you want to quit. We know...we've been there. Oftentimes you find yourself questioning the choice to foster or adopt. You whisper to yourself, "What was I thinking?" You feel isolated, alone, defeated, afraid, exhausted, angry, and overwhelmed. We're going talk about all this. But as you will see, hope is available.

Through all the trials of the foster and adoptive journey, I want you to know that the calling you've received to care for vulnerable children is valid. And it's beautiful. You are changing the world. You are flooding the darkness with light. And the hope that comes only from Jesus Himself is shining through you.

With hope for the journey,
Mike Berry

Part 1

You Are Not Alone

When three of Job's friends heard of the tragedy he had suffered, they got together and traveled from their homes to comfort and console him.

JOB 2:11 NLT

Beginning with Hope

Identifying Your Expectations and Apprehensions

Hope.

What a word—one of the most powerful words in the English language. Just seeing it printed on this page fills you with emotion, doesn't it? Perhaps a series of thoughts has raced through your mind in a matter of milliseconds since reading it.

Maybe you're just considering this journey of foster care or adoption, and you're hopeful as you dream of what could be. You've picked up this book just to get a better grasp on what you're getting yourself into. You've read articles, watched news reports, and read adoption blogs, trying to find that one word or phrase to finally convince you to take the plunge. Good for you—I wish I would have read a book like this 15 years ago.

Or perhaps you're well into this journey, and reading this word fills you with life. Your journey hasn't always been free and easygoing, but you feel alive. You've experienced deep peace and satisfaction in your life with your kiddos. Life isn't perfect, but you have an unshakable faith that God is in control and is holding your family together. The journey has been fairly easy for your family, and you see every day as another opportunity to live life to the fullest. Hope has not eluded you—it's wrapped itself around you like a warm blanket fresh out of the dryer.

On the other hand, you might still be searching. As you read the word "hope," you began squirming in your chair or shaking your head. You've run out of hope. The well is dry. You're in the longest, harshest desert you've ever walked through. You may even be regretting your decision to foster or adopt. You picked up this book as a last-ditch effort. Reading the word "hope" put a knot in your stomach because, unfortunately, hope has eluded you.

"Hope"—what a word! We all need it and everyone wants it, but it's often as elusive as a hummingbird. We lose it frequently or can't seem to find it when the journey becomes dark and challenging.

The Definition of the Journey

Most of us enter the adoptive or foster parenting journey with hope. And we're filled with passion and energy. For good reason too—we've been called to do this. We don't see it as a forced task but rather an invitation and a calling to go on an amazing adventure and change the lives of children who have come from difficult places. I'm willing to bet you entered this journey with a lot of excitement. You were ready to care for any child who was placed in your home or whose birth mother you were matched with. You didn't care what special need the child had—you were ready to love them regardless of the circumstances or story line. "Surely," you thought, "I can love them through whatever disorder, struggle, or issue they have! Surely that's enough to heal their wounds and lead them out of the darkness of their past."

So you jumped in with both feet. When the agency gave you a week to fill out the paperwork, you took a day. When your case manager sent you the schedule for training classes, you wrote them in bold print on the calendar and showed up 30 minutes early. You scoured Pinterest to find the perfect creative sign to tell your social media friends the big news that you were adopting.

Or if you adopted from the foster care system, you approached it with an overflowing heart to change the circumstances and future of vulnerable children. You eagerly awaited the arrival of your first placement. You prayed, and hoped, and dreamed. You stayed awake at night, staring at the ceiling because you couldn't get the picture of the children you saw on the Heart Gallery website out of your mind. The first time you laid eyes on the little girl or boy the case manager brought to your home, you gushed with love. You may have even cried. We did!

But it didn't take very long before you found yourself exhausted and out of gas. Six months or a year or two into your journey, you came to the realization that this was really, really tough. Navigating difficult relationships with your kids' birth parents. Managing relationships between your biological children and your foster or adopted children. Helping your kids understand what the word "adopted" means. Dealing with schoolyard bullies who target your adopted child.

> Six months or a year or two into the journey, you came to the realization that this was really, really tough.

Or worse—the sleepless nights because of the child who has night terrors, the fight for survival with a little girl with an unimaginably traumatic past, the food hoarding from a teenager who suffered periods of starvation early in his life, the urine-soaked underwear and rotting pull-ups stuffed in the back of a closet because a three-year-old girl was beaten by her birth dad for wetting. You were ill-prepared for the ways trauma manifests itself in everyday life. You had no idea just how deep these wounds go or even how to begin to help your kids through them. The constant battle has left you worn out.

Maybe the foster care system yanked you around like a yo-yo. You spent months being told one thing but having another happen. Perhaps you experienced a revolving door of case managers, and you couldn't get straight answers to your questions.

The special need *was* too much. The outbursts, fits of rage, acting out, violence, or extreme aggression threw your entire household into turmoil. Your extended family was no help either. They were even judgmental or harsh. "We told you this would happen," your dad barked at you while your child flipped out at his fifth birthday party because the candles on his cake were in the wrong place. Your mom chimed in with, "Adoption is a mistake!"

You never envisioned your parents saying such awful things to you. You believed the journey would be different. Maybe you even had a bit of a fantasy built up in your mind. But the three-year-old little girl you brought home from another country ten years ago is now a distant teenager, involved in toxic relationships with people who don't care about her.

Every day is filled with chaos, and it's all you can take. The constant pushing and pushing and pushing leaves you in shambles. What started off as hopeful has slowly become hopeless. Little by little the full tank of your heart leaked until it ran bone dry.

> You were never meant to travel this journey alone.

I understand. I see you. As I said earlier, I *am* you. I know how hopeless you feel because I've felt that way more times than I can remember in the past 15 years. So may I share something with you—from my heart to yours?

There is hope.

Let me say it again: There. Is. Hope.

"But Mike," you say, "you just described my journey perfectly. Every single heartbreaking moment. This isn't what I thought it would be—how in the world could there be any hope in the middle of these circumstances?"

I know, it's hard to believe. Trust me! I've felt that way many times over the years. But in the middle of the darkest storms of this journey, I've found hope. The reason? I know my children's stories are far from over. My story certainly didn't end when I was seven or eight or thirteen, and the same is true for my kids.

I also know that my family is held together by a loving Savior who will never let go of us. When we're tossed about in a desperate hurricane and we're feeling hopeless, Jesus shows up. Sometimes it's through an unexpected sense of peace, an encouraging thought that resonates with us, or a new insight that sheds light on our path. But often it's through other people who are on the same journey we are. We see and hear the words of Jesus through their words and actions. He leads us out of isolation and loneliness.

You were never meant to travel this journey alone. You were never meant to live in isolation. You were never meant to bear the brunt of your son's violent outbursts by yourself. You were never meant to carry the weight of your daughter's attachment issues single-handedly. You were never meant to stand alone against the cold, harsh winds of rejection from the child you brought home with love.

Through all of this, there is hope because Jesus is fighting with us and for us, even if it seems He's miles away. There is hope because

He brings supportive people into our lives at just the right time. Kristin and I have found this hope, and in the chapters that follow, you'll discover where it comes from.

Healing, restoration, and hope come from knowing and following Jesus. And He often works those wonders through the people who surround us and offer support. Jesus is the hope of the world. And He's the only one who can put the broken pieces of your family back together and bring healing and restoration to your hurting children. He willingly enters the wreckage of your life and this journey, and He holds you. He holds your children close and loves them through their trauma, their rage, and their fear. He is hope.

I know it's easier for me to type this than it is for you to believe it. Believe me, I know. But trust me—I'm not tossing out simplistic Christian rhetoric. I'm not trying to slap a Band-Aid on your deep wounds. I know how frustrating it is to be in the middle of a storm with your kids and have people quote Scripture or Christian clichés—even when they have no idea what this journey is like. It's not helpful. In fact, it's quite irritating.

I type these words because they've been true for us on our foster and adoptive journey. There's nothing (and I mean *nothing*) you could share about your own journey that would shock me. And there's nothing you could reveal (your thoughts, words, or actions) that would cause me to think less of you. We've been to the darkest places possible, including...

- constant rejection from a child we would move mountains to love and serve
- another child wanting to end her life at just 12 years old
- a child who routinely emotionally and physically attacks our family

- multiple run-ins with police with one of our kids (we know each of our local officers by name)
- judgmental stares, whispers, and glares from teachers, coaches, neighbors, and extended family
- feeling that we messed up, missed our calling, or failed as parents because we can't stop our children from making horrible choices

Yeah, we've been through all of it. And this is just the tip of the iceberg. It doesn't include the stuff we hide from most of the world.

In the middle of this, we have felt the embrace of a Savior who has promised to sit in the rubble with us. That's where we find hope. And He often deposits it into our lives through others. We find immense hope when human beings listen to us without flinching as we share some of the most ridiculous, messed-up, tragic stories from the trenches.

> Sometimes Jesus becomes the most real to us through other foster and adoptive parents who love us and accept us unconditionally.

We recently went through the ringer with one of our daughters. I'm stating this nicely. It was gut-wrenching. I could write an entire book on some of these moments. In the middle of this hurricane with our child (whom we love desperately), my wife, Kristin, pulled out her phone and called a close friend—an adoptive mother. I could hear a little of their conversation from the other room.

"I just need to talk to another person who knows exactly what we're going through and won't think less of our kid when I tell them what's going on." For the next 45 minutes I sat in the front room of our house, quietly listening to my child kick her wall and scream hateful words at us while Kristin talked it out with her friend. I ended up texting back and forth with a few of my close friends—fellow foster and adoptive dads. In the middle of the storm, while the wind and debris of our circumstance raged around us, we found hope. Jesus became as real as He's ever been because real flesh-and-blood human beings—with voices, feelings, and heartbeats—listened to us and quietly whispered, "Me too" as we poured our hearts out (see chapter 4).

We find ultimate hope and healing in Jesus. And that hope becomes real when it shows up through others.

Thankful for the Yes

In addition to finding hope through the people with whom we cross paths on this journey, we also find hope in saying yes to life—even when it doesn't make sense or seem possible. My family has been through many trials and tribulations on this journey, and you will read about some of them in this book. But those trials and tribulations will never overcome the power of us saying yes. Yes to more placements even when we were overwhelmed. Yes to a child who came from a major place of trauma. Yes to a teenage girl who had bounced from foster home to foster home. Yes to a sibling group who needed a forever home. Yes!

When I look back on our journey and remember the times we've said yes, I have to shake my head. On paper it didn't make sense. When our three youngest sons came to live with us through foster care, we already had five children (including two teenagers) living in our home. Our house was sizable, but it was shrinking very quickly. Most logical people would say, "Nah, that's too much. We've reached our limit." But the call to love vulnerable children often comes at the most unlikely times and in the most unlikely ways.

It may seem like an uphill climb, but there is much beauty involved. That beauty probably won't appear the moment you decide to step out and open your heart and home. Our family struggled to see the beauty for several years. We had to work through the reality of trauma with some of our children. We had to face hearings and visitations and continued cases, even when termination of parental rights was months overdue. It was frustrating and often defeating. But when I look back, I can see that it was also beautiful. As I watch my children play and discover and learn how to live life to the fullest, I am forever grateful that our hearts said yes even when our heads countered that the time wasn't right or we weren't ready.

An Unpredictable Journey

Winters in Cincinnati can be unpredictable and brutal. One day you're soaking up an unseasonable 80-degree day, donning shades and shorts, dreaming about summer...and the next? Well, it could be a frigid 15 and snowing sideways, just like that. "Unpredictable" is an understatement.

I grew up just east of the city in a little river town called New Richmond. I have thick skin for brutal winters. Cincinnati was a great city to grow up in. I have lots of fond memories. My family worked hard and played hard. My sister and I were never in any sort of need. We came from a pretty well-to-do background. Most of our cousins ended up at prestigious universities like Xavier, Arizona State, or the University of Cincinnati. We had successful, wealthy, and talented grandparents, aunts, uncles, and parents. It was custom in the Berry family to grow up, go to a good college, meet the perfect guy or girl, get married, take that fancy degree into the workplace, and after a few years, start filling our houses with miniature versions of ourselves. It's what I grew up with, it's what I saw firsthand, and it's what I'd decided the pathway of my life would look like, even as early as junior high.

That all changed one cold November night in 1998 during my senior year of college. I had just pulled in to a parking spot in front of our university library, shifted my beautiful metallic blue Pontiac Firebird into park, and leaned over for a good-night kiss from my brand-new fiancée, Kristin. We had been together for less than a year and were already planning to get married the following summer.

The wind was howling over the hilltop college campus of Cincinnati Christian University, where we attended. Snowflakes landed with a soft pat on the windshield of my car only to be dashed away quickly by the wipers swiping back and forth. I don't remember the exact temperature, but it was probably 20 degrees or colder that night.

As I looked over at my beautiful bride-to-be, I could tell something was on her mind. She had that look I had seen many times before over the past few months. It was either the result of an offhand comment I made earlier in the evening (a common occurrence) or a thought that suddenly crept up in her mind that needed to be released.

"What's wrong?" I asked, leaning back into my seat. She shook her head back and forth quietly. But I knew better than to let it go at that, so I persisted.

"Seriously, what's wrong? You look like something's on your mind."

"There is," she replied. "But I don't know if we should be talking about this or not."

"Well, try me," I said.

"Well, I've been thinking about us having kids someday and what that will look like."

"Okay…" I replied hesitantly.

"See, I knew I shouldn't bring this up. It's too early to talk about having kids," she retorted, shaking her head again and lowering her gaze.

"Babe, we're getting married in less than a year. Having kids is in

our future, so this is fair game. I don't mind. We can talk about it."
I grinned as she looked up at me.

"Okay," she continued, "I've been thinking about this a lot, and I think we should adopt all our kids."

Kristin's statement caught me completely by surprise, and my pleasant thoughts of someday starting a family screeched to a sudden stop. The conversation that unfolded between us over the next hour was as unpredictable as the Cincinnati weather.

"Well, why do you want to do that?" I asked, feeling a knot in my throat.

She replied, "My brother is adopted, my grandpa was in foster care...I don't know. It's just something I've always wanted to do. What about you?"

I wanted to blurt out a blunt NO! but tempered that. Our conversation had been cordial so far. Besides, I was the one who initiated it in the first place. What kind of a jerk would I have been if I suddenly squashed it?

> It wasn't that I was against adoption...I just didn't understand it.

It wasn't that I was against adoption...I just didn't understand it. After all, I grew up watching my older cousins get married and have babies. It's how everyone in my family came into the world, including me. The thought of two human beings producing another human being that resembled them—their features, mannerisms, ticks, and vocal inflections—was nothing short of amazing as far as I was concerned!

But being two firstborn children, Kristin and I couldn't stay entirely cordial, and an argument ensued.

"What's wrong?" she asked. "Now *you* have that look on your face that says something isn't okay."

"No, I'm fine," I replied a little sharply. "It's just that..."

My words trailed off, and she could definitely tell something wasn't right. I looked over at her and half smiled. The look on her face had turned a little more somber at this point.

"It's just that I wanted to have our children the old-fashioned way, you know? Like my entire family did. The thought of creating miniature people that look like you and me is so cool. I've dreamed of doing that since I was a little boy."

"Okay...well...I don't know if I want to build our family like that," she said.

I was stunned. Though it's hard to imagine now, I had simply assumed every woman on earth wanted to be a biological mother. At our small university, lots of students met, got married, and starting having babies. I was a little enthralled with the idea myself. So naturally, when I met my bride-to-be, I assumed she wanted to be a mother—the old-fashioned way.

And it gets even worse. I hate to admit this, but I also assumed that people chose adoption only because they couldn't have kids biologically.

In the nearly two decades since we had that conversation that night, I've discovered three things that have been obvious to many other people. First, not every woman grows up dreaming of becoming a mother. Letting go of that stereotype, I could appreciate the fact that each woman has a unique dream and calling.

Second, a growing number of women who *do* want to be mothers, *don't* want to be pregnant or to give birth. That's certainly not difficult to understand!

And third, many women choose adoption because they want to provide a home for children who don't have one, rather than bring more children into the world.

My wife fits those last two points. She was familiar with adoption—her brother came from an orphanage in Bulgaria, and her grandfather grew up in foster care. The reason she, too, wanted to adopt was that she didn't want to be pregnant or give birth. She told me matter-of-factly, "I don't want to be out of control of my body." I'm sorry to say, I argued with her back then. Oh, how I wish I could go back in time and tell my young and naive self what I believe now.

It's completely normal and acceptable for someone to feel this way. No law says a woman must be pregnant and give birth to be a mother. I had to experience a major paradigm shift, but that was my problem, not Kristin's. It took me some time to accept this, but I sure am glad I did. For my wife's sake and for mine. Today I know many families who have chosen adoption and many women who have felt the same way Kristin did almost 20 years ago.

After Kristin dropped that bombshell in the car that cold winter night, we sat and stared at each other for several minutes trying to figure out what to say next. In both of our minds was a question. "How could I end up with someone who has such different opinions about raising children?"

And it wasn't just having children or raising a family; it was everything. On paper we were nearly polar opposites. Our pre-marriage counselor confirmed this, as did many of our friends. We heard it over and over again. "You guys are so great together, but goodness gracious, are you different!" We knew it too. There wasn't a day that passed without us disagreeing over something. This night was no different. We argued back and forth for the next hour, hashing out our perspectives on having children, disciplining children, what kind of school we wanted them to attend...and we hadn't even said "I do" yet.

Eventually we became too tired to continue the battle. And our campus security had given us the final warning for curfew. (Small Christian universities often have rules like this.) So we called it a night and said the obligatory "I love you," followed by a kiss (two things you must do after an argument, even if you're not feeling it at the moment).

We were suddenly at odds over a topic that was supposed to be happy and fun to discuss. And frankly, it was my fault!

Fear

As I mentioned, it wasn't that I was against adoption; I just didn't understand it. But there was more at play within me than a lack of understanding. I was afraid. Fear was driving my perspective and causing me to speak the way I spoke to Kristin that night in my car. I was afraid of so many things back then. I was afraid of failure, afraid of feeling isolated, afraid of being uncomfortable, afraid of losing my identity, and afraid of dealing with the issues I saw in the foster and adopted kids I grew up with.

As soon as Kristin said the word "adopt," my mind flashed back to the fourth grade and a classmate named Jeff. He was disruptive, aggressive, and out of control. He had been removed from his biological family by the Department of Child Services and placed in foster care with a family in our school district.

> I didn't want to be the parent who was called every single day to come and retrieve my child because he or she was completely out of control.

Nearly every day Jeff had to be excused from the class and sent to the principal's office. His departure was commonly laced with expletives, a door slamming, and wall hangings falling to the floor. Our teacher did her best to hide the tears welling up in her eyes. She was at a loss, embarrassed, and frustrated.

I was afraid of being stuck with a kid like Jeff. That was the image I had in my mind when I thought about adoption and foster care. I didn't want to be the parent who was called every single day to come and retrieve my child because he or she was completely out of control. I had a much more pleasant scenario in my mind's eye than that when it came to raising a family.

On the other hand, I had a college class with a girl named Nikka who was being raised by wonderful foster parents. Nikka was the opposite of Jeff, and her parents cared for her as though she were theirs permanently. Even so, I was still afraid. I resisted even the notion of foster care or adoption. Whenever I wondered what adoption or foster care would look like, I was filled with dread that I would be stretched beyond my limit. I just didn't want to feel like that.

Fear is a tricky emotion. It is the primary tool that our enemy, Satan, uses to disrupt our lives (more about this later). He uses fear to convince us either not to move forward or to retreat to a safer place. His means for doing so are sneaky and often unnoticed until much later. As John Eldredge explains in his book *Wild at Heart*, Satan, the father of lies, sabotages our voices, our minds, and our perspectives, using them against us.

It's a brilliant move by the enemy when you think about it. He whispers thoughts of fear to us using our own voice. We recognize our own voice, we listen to it, and we believe it because we think we are doing the talking.

So fear gripped me. That's why I was resistant to adoption and foster care. I would hear my internal voice saying, "It's too risky. If you decide to do this, you'll surely fail. This is not what you had planned for your life! You're supposed to make lots of money and have a perfect family. Adoption screws up all of that! Think about what *you* want." The more the enemy spoke, the closer I listened. And the deeper I bought in to the lies.

Perhaps you can relate to this. Fear may be keeping you from deciding to go ahead and adopt or be a foster parent. If so, it's important that you remember this: You are not alone. You are normal.

Where's the Hope?

So, if fear is so common, how can we find hope?

Here's the answer: God Himself is at work in the background of our lives. I had no idea at the time, but as I look back, I see this clearly. He is always at work, even when it doesn't seem like it. For as much as I've learned how the enemy works to destroy us, I've also learned how much God works for us. He's in the pit of our lives with us.

And He's also at work outside of the pit on our behalf. That's good news because as I sat in the pit of my own fear and resistance that frigid November night, listening to the enemy's lies, God was orchestrating something more beautiful than I could have dreamed. I thought I knew how our story would unfold, what our new life together would tell, but God had something much more amazing in mind. It's been the furthest thing from perfect or peaceful or easy, but it's beautiful. It's perfectly imperfect.

I continually return to Isaiah 40:28-31:

> Do you not know?
>   Have you not heard?
> The LORD is the everlasting God,
>   the Creator of the ends of the earth.
> He will not grow tired or weary,
>   and his understanding no one can fathom.
> He gives strength to the weary
>   and increases the power of the weak.
> Even youths grow tired and weary,
>   and young men stumble and fall;
> but those who hope in the LORD
>   will renew their strength.
> They will soar on wings like eagles;
>   they will run and not grow weary,
>   they will walk and not be faint.

And that's why I know beyond a shadow of a doubt that there is hope. There is hope when this journey takes the life out of us. There is hope when we continue to love our broken children but they keep pushing us away and pursuing superficial or even toxic relationships. There is hope when the foster care system offers zero support and we're so exhausted we can't see straight. There is hope. Read that again: There. Is. Hope!

In this book, we're going to focus on two things: the hope we have in Jesus alone, and the way that hope usually comes—through finding others you can lean on during this journey. We believe that when Jesus gives us the gift of His presence and the gift of hope, He usually does it through others who come into our lives at just the right time.

> When Jesus gives us the gift of His presence and the gift of hope, He usually does it through others who come into our lives at just the right time.

I completely understand what it's like to enter into this journey with a full heart, but then to realize how defeating and dark it can be at times. I know what it's like to walk—no, crawl—through this trench, wondering if life will ever get easier, if we'll ever find a way out, if our child will ever respond to us in a healthy way, if there is any hope.

You are not alone—I'm right there with you. Let's talk.

Your Turn

Take some time with your husband or wife or a close friend and talk about these questions: "When I think of adoption or foster care..."

1. What do I feel hopeful about?

2. What am I afraid of? What keeps me up at night?

3. What has left me feeling defeated, isolated, or weary?

4. What have I already experienced on this journey that is good?

What Am I Getting Myself Into with Foster Care?

1. *It's an adventure*—of epic proportions. You can (and should) do a ton of research, but you cannot completely avoid the element of the unknown. One thing you can be sure of is that you will experience huge ups and downs on a weekly basis.

2. *There will be frustration.* You'll be told one thing, and then another thing will happen. Your child's case may get pushed back another few months. Even if parental rights should have been terminated, visits with birth parents will continue. Going into this process with eyes wide open is the best approach.

3. *You will grow.* Kristin and I are wiser after eight years of foster parenting. We've learned so much about ourselves, and the process has been extremely valuable. Our perspective on parenting has been shaped by extreme trials. We wouldn't trade this growth.

4. *The children placed in your care may be difficult.* Commercials for foster care and adoption often sugarcoat reality. Don't be lured into believing you're on a rescue mission or you're a superhero. The children in your care need someone to love them for who they are and to stay consistent with them through extreme circumstances. Their difficult backgrounds will produce a myriad of struggles in your home.

5. *The system is difficult to understand and navigate.* The foster care system is backlogged with huge caseloads and high turnover rates among workers. Many case managers are overworked and underpaid. You may go through several case managers in a few years. You'll receive timelines or details that may be inaccurate. When a child was placed in our home for just a weekend or for a week or two, that usually turned into a month or more. Three of our children never left. And we're quite thankful for that!

6. *You need a support system.* Your support should not come from your case manager or anyone in the court system—in other words, people whose loyalty must be divided. Rather, you need other foster parents who are on the journey with you, including some seasoned pros.

7. *You will learn how to love unconditionally.* You'll learn what unconditional love *should* look like. The choice to put it into practice is yours to make.

2

Jumping Off

The Joy and Struggle of Choosing This Journey

I stand on the edge of a cliff with my toes bending over the rocky ledge. The sun is high in the sky, with no clouds for miles. Birds zoom back and forth over the green waters of the lake. In the trees behind me, cicadas chirp an eerie harmony—the sound of summer in the Midwest.

Twenty-five feet below me, the murky green water laps, beckoning me to step off and take the plunge. I look out and see my wife treading water. We've determined the spot is safe, and she's already mustered the courage to jump. So have several kids in our youth group who are much younger than me. A few of them stand behind me, cheering me on. The boys, of course, jeer me and jokingly call me a coward. I silence them with a wave of my index finger.

I fear the unknown. I've never swum in this lake before, and a million what-ifs race through my mind. "What if I hurt myself when I hit the water? What if I can't get out? What if there's a snake? After all, they have water moccasins in these parts."

Fear after fear after fear pile up like logs jamming the flow of a mountain stream, preventing me from stepping off. They're keeping me from the thrill of something I've never done before. My sense of adventure is crippled, and I want to step back from the edge.

But just then, something leaps in my heart and I suddenly step off, flying through the air for what seems like forever. Shrubs on the opposite cliff flash past in a blur as I plummet 25 feet down. I hear my students whoop.

My bare feet make contact with the surface of the cool water, and I disappear beneath the ripples. My first feeling is warmth. The hot July sun has warmed the water to bathtub temperatures. But as my 185-pound body dives deeper, I feel the deep coolness of the dark waters below. My eyes open as my body ceases to go any farther. I extend my arms and begin to swim to the surface. When my head appears above the water, everyone cheers wildly. These junior high kids never thought their youth pastor would take the plunge.

> Oftentimes it's not the initial jump that wears you out, but continuing to jump over and over.

I glance over at my wife, who's still treading water. She smiles. "That was fun," I think to myself. "I'm ready to do it again." And so I do. Again and again and again until I'm almost too tired to climb up the trail to the top of the cliff. Oftentimes it's not the initial jump that wears you out, but continuing to jump over and over.

Beginnings

Once I had wrapped my mind around the idea of adoption—questioning some of my unexamined assumptions and identifying the source of my fear—I gradually began to warm up to the idea. Some friends from church who had adopted from China heard that we were considering adoption, so they invited us to an hour-long introductory meeting with Families Through International Adoption.

The thought of a child living in an orphanage or on the streets without a mom or dad saddened me. We eventually decided to proceed with international adoption and began filling out the mountain of paperwork.

The next step was to meet with a local adoption agency in town. After that, a representative would meet with us at our home to make sure our physical environment was satisfactory for a child.

We walked into Adoption Support Center in Indianapolis on a frigid day in February. It was a tiny Victorian-style house in a trendy Northside area of Indianapolis known as Broadripple. A friendly woman named Mavis greeted us warmly, offered us water and coffee, and then led us upstairs to a cozy room. Kristin and I sat close to each other on a soft love seat. We were both a little nervous.

While Mavis retreated to the offices downstairs to gather our folder with the necessary paperwork, we sat hand in hand, looking out the picture window over the community. As the minutes ticked by, we became more and more nervous. We later laughed about that because we really had no reason to fear. Neither one of us had ever committed a crime. We were never in jail, although I had been detained by the police when I was in high school (another story for another book). We made enough money and owned a beautiful little farmhouse in a community just north of Indianapolis in the suburbs. Still, for some reason, we were worried.

Mavis returned and began the interview. Her warm, calm demeanor put us at ease. As she talked in her soothing tone, our anxiety level dropped. For the first 20 minutes or so, she asked general questions: "Tell me about your families growing up." "Did you get along with your parents and siblings?" "How long have you been married?" Then came the big one: "Why do you want to adopt?" Now that we were at ease, we could answer each question with confidence and poise. Then she asked us a question that caused us to stop and think. "May I ask why you want to adopt internationally?"

We looked at each other. "Well, we just figured that's what everyone does when they adopt," I replied.

Mavis smiled and closed our folder. "Have you considered domestic adoption? We do those here too, and we have a three-month average turnaround on placements. And it's much less expensive."

Kristin leaned in, hungry for more information. Suddenly, Jeff appeared in my mind, and an old knot returned to my stomach.

Mavis went on to explain the process. With the help of the Adoption Support Center, we would collect pictures of ourselves, our home, our dogs, and our community to create a family biography. The biography would then be shown to expectant women who were looking to place their children for adoption.

Looking back, I can see that even in my excitement, I still hadn't yet taken adoption seriously. For some reason, I never thought it would really happen. But suddenly, when Mavis explained we could complete a domestic adoption in only three months, the idea became more real to me than it had ever been. That afternoon we walked out of Adoption Support Center with our heads spinning.

Even though I remained apprehensive, the cost difference had at least started me thinking. After talking it over for a week, we decided to move forward with a domestic adoption. Inside, I was still dragging my feet a little, but the journey had begun. We were going to be parents.

Jump First, Question Later

In my 40 years of existence here on earth, I've learned an important life lesson: When you decide to step out and do something risky, such as adopting a child, life starts moving fast. You feel as if you've just jumped to lightspeed. You wonder whether you made the right choice, and you reminisce about the days before you made the decision, often thinking, "If only I could return to that day and tell myself a few things about this journey..."

> When you do decide to step out and do something bold and risky, such as adopt or foster, you have no idea how God will use that for kingdom purposes.

But I've also learned this: When you do decide to step out and do something bold and risky, such as adopt or foster, you have no idea how God will use that for kingdom purposes. You have no idea what story He will choose to tell through your choice. We'll talk more about this later, but let that thought marinate for a moment, especially if you're apprehensive or fearful.

Perhaps you've already adopted or you're currently on the foster care journey, and you're second-guessing your decision or even wishing you could go back. Let me encourage your heart with these two truths:

1. As we have seen, yours is a story of hope. Your heavenly Father is with you, and He's *for* you. He is the author of your story.

2. You have no idea how God can and will use your journey to tell the world a bigger story of hope, compassion, and love. We cannot see into the future, but we can depend on God, trusting that He is accomplishing His purpose in us and through us.

I wish I would have understood these two truths in 2002. Even though we had decided to go on this adventure together, I constantly battled fear. I was such a self-centered, arrogant person back then! Even though others saw me as servant-minded, I was looking for ways to serve me. I had no idea how big the story God was preparing to tell through our family really was.

> I had no idea how big the story God was preparing to tell through our family really was.

On April 27, 2002, we loaded up a few vans full of volunteer youth leaders at the church I served as youth pastor, and we headed for Westside Indianapolis for a training event. We laughed and joked and sipped our coffee as we zoomed down the expressway. It was a warm, spring morning—the kind that gets you excited for summer to finally arrive. I had no idea that our lives were about to change forever.

As the cheerful chatter continued, I felt my cell phone buzz. Back then, Kristin and I shared a cell phone because there was no such thing as a family plan with discounted rates. Besides, it was just the two of us. We always went everywhere together, so there was no need for more than one cell phone. I pulled the buzzing device out of my pocket and saw a number I didn't recognize. But it had an Indianapolis area code, so I answered.

"Hello."

"Hi, is this Mike?" a woman said.

"Yes, I'm Mike."

"Mike, this is Martina from Adoption Support Center. I just want you to know that I am en route to Wishard Memorial Hospital in downtown Indianapolis. Tira has gone into labor. Your baby girl should be coming anytime in the next few hours."

My baby girl?

I nearly dropped the phone, speechless. We had never met Tira, the birth mother, but a month and a half earlier, she had reviewed our family biography and had chosen us to adopt her baby. Of course, we had seen this day coming, but here it was, right before us at a moment's notice.

Elated, Kristin grabbed the phone and wrote down all the pertinent details. I sat in the van seat, stunned. When we arrived at the venue for the training event, our life-long friends John and Nicole let us borrow their minivan to drive to the hospital. As I was walking out the door, one of my youth leaders looked at me and asked, "Are you ready for this?" I could only shake my head back and forth. Still no words.

> We had planned for this, and the adoption agency equipped and coached us, but nothing could have fully prepared us for this moment.

The day became a whirlwind. Our daughter Jaala was born at 2:32 p.m. on April 27, 2002. She was a perfectly healthy baby girl and slept soundly in our arms. I was the first person to feed her, and my wife was the first to change her diaper.

We couldn't believe it. We were overnight parents. Our life was now on a different track. We no longer had only ourselves to look after, but also a tiny baby. We had planned for this, and the adoption agency equipped and coached us, but nothing could have fully prepared us for this moment. We didn't have nine months to talk about it and make decisions. We had suddenly come face-to-face with reality.

Jim Daly, president of Focus on the Family, once asked me in a radio interview, "What would you tell people, particularly men, who are apprehensive or afraid to go on the adoption journey?"

Without hesitation I answered, "Jump off!"

Even amid your fear, if you know this is what you're called to do, jump off. Take a step of obedience that feels completely crazy and trust that your heavenly Father will fill in the blanks. If the fear is enormous, then perhaps you need to pump the brakes a little, spend some time in prayer, consult with veterans (those who have gone before you and have the scars to prove it), and even wait if the timing isn't right. There's nothing wrong with that. The last thing you would ever want to do is move into a major life decision hastily. But most importantly, don't let fear stand in the way of doing something you know in your heart you are supposed to do.

> Sometimes your highest calling scares you the most.

In 2002, that's what I decided to do. There was no looking back. There was no changing our minds. Even in the middle of my fear and apprehension, I knew deep down that we were called to do this. Sometimes your highest calling scares you the most.

———

I stand on the edge of the cliff with my toes bending over the rocky ledge of life. The sun is high in the sky, with no cloud for miles. All around me, the murky waters of this life lap at me, beckoning me to step off the ledge and take the plunge. I'm terrified, but something about the adventure draws me in. I look out and see my wife treading water. She's already mustered the courage to jump. She's off and running. And so I jump.

The Adoption Process

What does the adoption process look like? Great question. Here's a quick rundown of what to expect.

Domestic Adoption

This is any adoption that takes place in the country where you live. The cost can be as low as $12,500 but often ranges from $25,000 to $50,000 if you work with an agency. This includes some living expenses for the birth mother, fees for a home study, attorney fees, and a few other miscellaneous costs.

Families may choose to do a private adoption with just a lawyer. This will save on cost, but there is more risk. Believe it or not, adoptions transacted outside of credible agencies with solid screening processes are sometimes scams—even if a lawyer is involved. We never recommend responding to want ads or advertisements in a local newspaper or on websites like Craigslist.

Domestic adoption is usually faster than international adoption or foster-to-adopt, averaging four to twelve months. Of course, it can take much longer than that in some cases. Children are usually placed at birth.

International Adoption

This is any adoption that takes place outside of the country where you live. People commonly adopt from China, Ethiopia, India, and South Korea. However, there are many other countries that are open to this process. The average cost is usually between $50,000 and $100,000, which includes travel expenses, various agency fees, specific country expenses, and home study costs.

International adoptions can take from twelve months to four years. Each country is different when it comes to the ages of the children who are available for adoption, their legal status, the involvement of their birth families, and so on.

Foster-to-Adopt

This is any adoption that occurs through the foster care system. People who choose this option must go through foster care training and then indicate their desire to provide a foster-to-adopt home. This can be a very long and drawn-out process, taking from two to four years. However, the financial costs are minimal.

To learn more about the process of adoption, you can ask us questions through our website, www.confessions ofanadoptiveparent.com.

Learning to Swim

What to Do When
You're In Over Your Head

Jumping is one thing. Swimming is another thing entirely.

If you're confident you've been called to the foster or adoption journey, I suggest you do what we did—jump first, question later. But once you've jumped, you do need to ask your questions and find some answers. And you need to ask the right people. That's what we're going to talk about in this chapter.

On the adoptive and foster care journey, you quickly learn the difference between jumping and swimming.

In one sense, jumping is the easy part. You step off your perch and let gravity do the rest. Sure, you need to make sure your body is straight, your toes are pointed downward, your arms are at your side, and you're holding your breath. But really, it's pretty cut and dried. Just follow a simple technique to avoid pain, a waterlogged nose, or a headache for the rest of the day.

Swimming, on the other hand, takes much more effort than jumping does. Anyone can jump, but not everyone can swim.

Jumping into the foster care and adoptive journey was relatively easy. Many people had told us that we could do it, that our family was made for this. We even had a group of people cheering us on. Most people think the idea of adoption or foster care is great. Close friends, people in your small group, relatives, neighbors...these people may become your mini fan club when you begin this journey.

> They were cheering us for jumping. They weren't teaching us to swim.

That was our experience—everyone applauded our decision and hailed us for taking this step. (I may have taken on the hero complex once or twice.) People who heard about our decision would stand up and cheer. We also had the support of fellow adoptive and foster parents.

But as we'll see, they were cheering us for jumping. They weren't teaching us to swim.

Growth Spurt

Just a few years after we began the journey, our family had grown quite a bit. As we surveyed the landscape of our life, we realized we were almost complete. We had decided it was just about time to end our foster care license and focus on the story God was telling through us. In just nine short years, we had gone from a family of three to a family of ten. You read that right—ten!

Two years after our first daughter was born in 2002, we became foster parents of two siblings whose birth mother had requested they be placed with us. Talk about a sudden change! We'd had one child who slept through the night, rarely made a fuss, and pretty much always cooperated with us. Suddenly we were caring for three children who had different sleeping patterns, and two of them had come from a home filled with trauma. It was a shock to our system. We were apprehensive but excited—and we had no idea what we were getting into. At the time, I was a full-time youth pastor. The adoption occurred in the summer, when I was on the road with our students at various retreats, camps, conferences, and training events for nearly two solid months. My wife took care of the three children pretty much on her own. Looking back, I can't believe we made it through that season. If divorce had ever been a possibility, it would have been during that summer. (I'm kidding...sort of.) My wife is clearly an angel in a human body, and she gives more grace than any other person on earth.

It was a stressful time. Soon after the two children came into our care, we learned that they probably wouldn't be heading back into their birth mother's care again. In March 2008, we finalized their adoption.

As our family grew from five to ten, the crazy journey was filled with ups and downs and twists and turns. To say we were exhausted would be an understatement. We often didn't know which way was up. We attended hearings, had case manager visits, and endured outbursts from kids when their parents blew off visitations.

We also received a diagnosis of alcohol-related neurodevelopmental disorder (ARND) for a few of our children. In layman's terms, it means they were exposed to drugs and alcohol before they were born. They would never recover from the effect on their brains. Our oldest son had an especially hard time. His violent outbursts and daylong temper tantrums caused so much disruption in our household, we were often holding on by a thread. Many times I whispered in my heart and mind, "This isn't the way it was supposed to be."

Four years later we were at our wits' end. We were drowning! At times, we were struggling to keep our heads above the waves. We had jumped in with both feet years earlier. But we soon realized that we were floundering and reaching out for help that often wasn't there.

> We realized pretty quickly that we were floundering and reaching out for help that wasn't there.

The View from the Shore

It wasn't long after we began the journey that we realized a discrepancy. Lots of people—fellow foster and adoptive parents, members of our church, and other friends—had told us, "Jump off. Do it. Take the old plunge into foster care and adoption. Don't ask questions; just jump in and rely on God to provide everything for you." This seemed a bit rash at the time, but the justification was legit: "If you're called to do this, then do it." We were confident we were called, but we quickly noticed that once we had taken the plunge, most of the voices that had encouraged us to jump first and ask questions later were much quieter when we found ourselves drowning and in need of help.

My friend Andrew has a great illustration for this very thing. He says that we are good at telling people to jump off the edge. Picture it as a couple stepping to the edge of a pier out over the ocean. When they get near the edge and prepare to jump, those of us who are already on the adoption journey often say, "Go for it! Jump!" Then we take our place on the shoreline to watch them take the plunge. We cheer and hoot and holler as the couple grab hands, gaze into each other's eyes, whisper "I love you," step off the edge, and plummet down to the cool waters below.

We celebrate like mad as we watch them take the plunge. We

cheer as if our favorite football team had just intercepted the ball in the last seconds of the game and had run it back for the go-ahead touchdown, sealing a victory. We're head-over-heels excited for them.

But while we're on the shoreline high-fiving, hugging, and celebrating our dear friends' decision to jump into the foster or adoptive journey, we miss something. Out beyond the pier, the surf has picked up. Winds are starting to blow, riptides are forming, and whitecaps are slapping against the pier. Our couple—once joyful, excited, and determined—is becoming panicked, fearful, and desperate.

Someone on the shoreline realizes they're in trouble and begins to get the others' attention. A voice from the back of the celebration says, "Hey, it doesn't look like they're doing too well out there in the water. Maybe we should help?" She looks around at everyone standing next to her on the shoreline, but no one says a word. A few people fold their arms and begin to look at the sandy beach beneath their feet. It's almost as if they're ignoring the reality before their eyes.

Suddenly another person in the group on the shore thinks he can hear the couple saying something. He steps toward the edge of the water, leans out, and cups his hands over his right ear. Then he turns, cups both of his hands over his mouth, and yells, "Whhhaaatttt?"

Faintly the onlookers hear the couple yell back, "Tell us what to do—we don't know how to swim!"

Everyone onshore looks at each other, perplexed. A few people shrug and hold their hands out to their side with palms open. Meanwhile, the waves are growing, the clouds are darkening, lightning flashes, and thunder rolls.

No one told the couple about the trauma children carry with them when they are bounced from foster home to foster home—15-foot swell! The new parents were unaware that separation from a birth parent can cause extreme attachment issues—whitecap! They didn't know his drug and alcohol exposure at birth would cause increasingly difficult behavior and impulsivity—lightning!

The crowd of onlookers are at a loss. One person in the back weaves through the group with a concerned look on his face. At the water's edge, he peers out to see our new adoptive couple really struggling now. He too cups his hand over his ear to better hear their cries for help: "Help us—we don't know how to swim! What should we do?"

With that, the man on the shoreline yells back, "We only know how to tell you to jump. We don't know how to tell you to swim!"

If you're in the water, here's what I want you to know.

This book is *not* written by people standing on the shoreline. When you cry out, "I don't know how to swim," we're not going to tell you, "We just know how to tell you to jump." This book is written from one perspective: *We are in the water right next to you, fighting to stay above the waves along with you.*

Or picture us as Coast Guard rescuers who are lowered down into the water with you. Just as the rescuers won't leave your side until you're safe, we're not going to leave your side until you're in a better place mentally, spiritually, and physically.

My situation may not be that different from yours. I'm raising children who have big-time special needs. I'm in the water, being tossed around by whitecaps. I have scars on my heart and up and down my body from my children's extreme behavior. After I jumped off the cliff, I realized I couldn't swim, and I was drowning.

I've wanted to give up on this whole foster and adoptive journey a time or two. But I found my way to safety. I found hope.

But How?

You're probably wondering how I could find hope in such a stormy situation. If you're out in the waves and wondering what in the world you should do to get through this choppy season, try these four things. They helped us!

Acknowledge your circumstance. I don't know why, but for whatever reason, we human beings have a bad habit of denying the trouble we find ourselves in. We default to isolation because we think that will make us feel better. "If I just keep this to myself and not let anyone know I'm drowning," we reason with ourselves, "then everything will be okay." Sounds ridiculous, doesn't it? Yet this is what Kristin and I have done, and you probably have too at times on this journey. There is refreshing release when we can simply raise our hand and say, "I need help—my circumstances are not good right now."

> There is refreshing release when we can simply raise our hand and say, "I need help."

Reach out for hands around you. You may feel as if you're alone on this journey, but the truth is, you're not. We'll focus on this in chapter 8, but for now, I'll simply tell you, you're not alone. When you take a moment to wipe some of the surf out of your eyes and look around you, you'll see lots and lots of other families floundering around you, struggling through the same predicament. Reach out for them. You may not find solutions for your out-of-control child's situation or a disorder that holds your entire family captive, but you will find

> Camaraderie brings some of the greatest healing.

strength, encouragement, and comfort. Camaraderie brings some of the greatest healing.

Share the lifeboat. I once read the story of a lifeboat carrying passengers from the ill-fated *Titanic* who were rowing away from the sinking ship but then decided to go back and fill their boat to capacity. Doing so would put them dangerously close to the floundering ship, whose massive hull could have pulled them under as it disappeared below the waves. They saved 20 to 30 more people by taking this risk.

All of us have learned and grown through our life experience on this amazing, difficult, beautiful, and tragic parenting journey. We must stay committed to pulling others up out of the waves. And if you're floundering in the waves right now, you must be willing to be pulled up.

> We remind parents not to base their children's future on their current behavior.

Believe in a brighter day. I know this sounds like a line from a cheesy Hallmark card. Trust me—I am *not* into being cheesy, so I hesitated suggesting it. But the truth is, there *is* a brighter day. We remind parents not to base their children's future on their current behavior. Why? Because God created everyone with purpose—including everyone in your family.

You may be in the waves of this journey for a while. Your circumstances might not change anytime soon, so you have to find hope in the middle of tough circumstances, not in spite of them or outside of them. That's the reality of life. The way you find that hope is to believe in a brighter day ahead.

We've seen that our greatest healing is likely to come through those who are on the journey with you. In the next chapter, we'll take a look at how that works.

The Health of Your Marriage Matters

Foster care and adoption take a toll on your marriage. Here's why.

1. *It takes all your time.* There's really no way to avoid this. You will have case conferences, visitations, placement hearings, doctor's appointments, therapy sessions...the list goes on.

2. *It steals all your emotion.* You probably joined the ranks of foster care because you have hearts as big as the Grand Canyon. When those first few placements came into your home, they drew all your emotion and left little for anything or anyone else—including each other.

3. *It piles on added stress.* This is obvious. But remember, as stress builds, other things will take a backseat, including hobbies, friendships, and even your marriage.

4. *It pits you against one another.* When you are sleep deprived, emotionally drained, and feeling defeated, you can easily start fighting more than you did before you became foster parents.

5. *It drains your energy.* You need energy to be intimate. You need energy even to desire sex. But foster parents often just long for one good night's sleep.

So how do you maintain your most important relationship while caring for the children who have been placed in your home?

1. *Plan ahead.* You and your spouse can't go on a date at the drop of a hat, but you can plan together to make this happen. Talk together about ways you can invest in the most important relationship you have—your marriage.

2. *Be intentional.* Follow through on your plan. Take action and seek out opportunities to rest and to revitalize your relationship. Pick up your phone and call for help. Talk to your case manager. Circle your date night or weekend getaway on the calendar and guard it fiercely. Being intentional is the only way to make sure your plans will succeed.

3. *Be strategic.* Use the resources that are available. Respite providers can care for your kids while you rest.

4. *Be consistent.* We know the value of consistency in training children, but being consistent in marriage enrichment also pays big dividends. A one-and-done date night or one lunch date during the workweek won't cut it. Your marriage can become healthier even amid the challenges of foster parenting, but you must consistently invest in it.

The future of your family depends on the health of your marriage. Making this a priority is the best thing you can do for each other and for your kids.

4

Me Too

Finding Strength in Relationships

I travel a lot. I'm often boarding a plane to another city to speak to foster and adoptive parents about hope and the power of camaraderie.

Not long ago I was in New York City, speaking to a large group of adoptive parents. I had no idea New York City had such a large population of adoptive parents, but it does. It was inspiring to be with the beautiful people from each of the surrounding boroughs.

One particular woman grabbed my heart. Except for the fact that she adopted internationally and all of our adoptions were domestic, her story lined up almost exactly with ours. She was dealing with her daughter's attachment issues, defiance, and daily battles—issues we were facing with some of our children. She attended both of my afternoon teaching sessions, and in them she shared her fears, struggles, anxieties, and exhaustion. At one point, she looked at me and said something that still rings in my mind:

"How did I end up here?"

"Exactly," I thought to myself as I listened to her heart. I knew precisely where she was coming from and what drives this question. It's hopelessness. It's a deep love for a child who constantly pushes you away. It's the loss of a dream you once had. Or simply an ideal morphing from what you thought this journey would be to what it actually has become. After years of journeying down a rough, rocky, treacherous path, you wake up and say to yourself, "How did I end up here?"

You realize you have to learn to cope with your new reality. Sure, you've made some great memories, but the ideal, the dream life you had conjured up when you first began this journey, now looks more like the twisted metal of a car crash or the piles of rubble after a massive earthquake. You wake up and find yourself sitting in the wreckage. It's the new normal. How do you find encouragement in the middle of this? How do you find others who are on this journey or at least understand you enough not to judge or criticize you when everything in your world begins to fall apart?

In January 2001 we moved from Cincinnati, Ohio, to Indianapolis, Indiana. For the first time in our lives, we were living away from our families. We were starting fresh with no friends and no support system. I had been hired by a church there, and building solid friendships was slow going at first. It took us a few months to adjust to a new city.

That all changed one November night when another young couple,

John and Nicole, invited us to their house for dinner. We were excited to join them. For the first time since moving to a new city, someone who was our age and in our stage of life wanted to spend time with us. Some kind elderly couples or families with two or more kids had taken us to lunch after church or invited us to their house for a meal, but we desperately needed to be with people we could relate to.

That first meal together would be the beginning of a beautiful friendship that continues to thrive today. John and Nicole came to the hospital and walked with us when our first daughter arrived suddenly in April 2002. They stood next to us few months later when the judge pronounced that we had officially adopted her. They brought us meals, cleaned our house, sat with us when we were so tired we couldn't think straight, and much more. They grieved with us in the spring of 2004 when the baby girl we were supposed to bring home as our second child passed away at birth. Later that year, when we welcomed home our first two foster placements, they were there next to us, encouraging us, praying for us, and helping us as much as they could.

When they began the adoption process a few years later, we returned the favors, even remodeling a room in their house so their brand-new baby would have her own room. In the years following, we've gone on vacations together, spent holidays together, watched each other's kids perform in musicals, sat in the ER with one another, cried together, grieved with one another, and walked through stages of life together.

Another couple, Ryan and Megan, have also become close friends and an integral part of our support system. They, too, have walked with us in the various ups and downs of this journey, as we have for them. When they became foster parents for the first time, we took them clothes, diapers, meals, and some Starbucks gift cards to help them recover from sleepless nights.

In fact, a few years ago, when I was fired from my job at a church in Indianapolis and we were considering our next steps as a family, one big reason we decided to stay put was to continue building our friendships with John and Nicole and Ryan and Megan. They are more than friends...they are like brothers and sisters to us.

> There's not a thing we could share with one another that would cause the other to be shocked or disappointed.

Our relationships with these four amazing people are snapshots of the power of community in adoption and foster care circles. We have walked the same path—fostering kids, adopting, and parenting children with major special needs. The most beautiful part of our friendship is that there's not a thing we could share with one another that would cause the other to be shocked or disappointed. There's no judgment, no criticism, only authenticity. There are times when we get together and completely unload our emotions with one another.

Sometimes our journey looks more like a crash-test dummy commercial than a Pottery Barn Christmas ad, and these four beautiful people are right there in the wreckage with us. When their journey becomes dark and difficult, we sit in the middle of the rubble with them. We are not afraid of the darkness, the wounds, or the frustration. No one is unwilling to enter the mess of the others' journey. We often sit across coffee shop tables or on the other end of our cell phone conversations, nodding and quietly saying, "Me too." As Brené Brown said in one of her astounding TED Talks, "The two most powerful words when we're in struggle: Me too."*

This is the type of community you must have on the foster or adoptive journey. In chapter 10, we'll consider how to formulate

---

* Listen to Brené's talk "Listening to Shame" at https://www.ted.com/talks/brene_brown_listen ing_to_shame.

a strong support community and how to find the right people for your support group. For now, here is a quick list of crucial qualities that our friendships with John and Nicole and Ryan and Megan have provided for us. Like us, you will need friends who are...

- nonjudgmental
- in the water, not standing on the shore (In other words, they are also foster or adoptive parents...usually. Every now and then, you find people who are not specifically on the journey but can be wonderful cheerleaders and supporters.)
- understanding
- willing to enter the wreckage

These are the people you want walking with you, especially when the journey becomes tough. Let's take a closer look at the fourth bullet.

With Friends like This...

The Old Testament book of Job is a fascinating story of how quickly everything can fall apart and become so devastating that your life feels like a thriller movie script or a tragic novel. Job's story goes like this...

He has a lot of money, a big family, lots of servants, lots of stuff, a ton of houses, servants, livestock (which was a big deal in that day and signified that you were loaded), and much more. We're talking about the Richard Branson or Elon Musk kind of rich and famous.

In chapter 1, Satan, the father of lies, wagers with God that Job is faithful to Him because He's given him so much nice stuff. But if his stuff were taken away, Satan says, Job would not be so faithful.

God responds, "You're on! Take all the stuff away from him—the family, the vacation homes, the wealth—but don't hurt him." Satan agrees and heads out as the most infamous home wrecker in history.

Everything is taken away from Job. In the blink of an eye he loses his servants, his homes, his family, his livestock...*everything!* Only his life remains.

Could you imagine being Job? Take a second and think about your entire life. Imagine your children, your home, your job, your pets, your material possessions, your friendships...everything that makes up your physical life here on earth. Do you have a warm place to sleep at night? Do you have access to transportation? Have you begun to accumulate a few possessions just for fun?

Okay, now imagine you left all of this one morning and headed to your workplace. You're driving along, maybe sipping your latte and listening to the morning news, but as you pull into the parking lot at work, your coworker Joe comes running out to your car, clearly distraught.

"Mike, I hate to have to tell you this, but...it's your children...they were killed in a storm. I'm so sorry, man. And your house...it was demolished, and all your stuff...it's gone."

"Umm...*what*?" This would be the point where I collapse to the floor in a puddle of tears. It's such an unbelievable circumstance that even as I type these words I can't wrap my mind around loss so deep.

How would you feel? Devastated? Lost? Hopeless? Probably all of this and way more than you can imagine. I have no idea how I would react to hearing that everything I know and love is suddenly gone, just like that, but I can tell you it wouldn't be pretty.

Amazingly, Job remains faithful.

But then, to the reader's (and Job's!) bewilderment, we enter round two. Satan wagers with God that Job is *still* praising His name only because Job has retained his health and his dashing good looks. But mess with those, Satan says, and Job will surely turn on God.

Again, God takes the bet, and excruciatingly painful sores break out all over Job's body.

But just in time, we come to one of the best parts of Job's story. In fact, this is one of my favorite moments in the entire Bible because it illustrates the power of community. After everything has fallen apart on Job, after he's lost everything he owns and loves, and after he is infected with the terrible skin disease, this happens:

> When three of Job's friends heard of the tragedy he had suffered, they got together and traveled from their homes to comfort and console him. Their names were Eliphaz the Temanite, Bildad the Shuhite, and Zophar the Naamathite. When they saw Job from a distance, they scarcely recognized him. Wailing loudly, they tore their robes and threw dust into the air over their heads to show their grief. Then they sat on the ground with him for seven days and nights. No one said a word to Job, for they saw that his suffering was too great for words (Job 2:11-13 NLT).

Job's three friends got together and traveled from their homes to comfort and console him.

When they saw Job, they showed their grief by tearing their robes and throwing dust over themselves.

And then they sat on the ground with him for seven days and nights, *saying nothing*!

Now, let's not jump ahead in the story. We know Job's friends won't turn out to be the perfect counselors, but let's give them credit for their actions so far. They came to him, they identified with him, and they sat with him.

I don't know about you, but this is what I need friends to do when my life falls apart. At this point, Job's friends are acting like the people I want to lean on, depend on, or call on when my life turns dark.

You've probably figured out by now that the adoptive and foster care journey can be just that at times—dark. It can leave you feeling defeated, even devastated. It's far from easy. In fact, it can drain the life out of you, just as if you were told that everything you knew, loved, and held sacred was suddenly gone. It can leave you feeling pretty desperate.

We begin this journey without really understanding how it will turn our lives upside down. How could we know? This is new territory. No one could have predicted how beautiful and how difficult it would be.

But now you're a few years in, and you take a moment to survey the landscape of your life. Some moments you wouldn't trade for the world. Others...well, they're not what you bargained for. This is a critical moment—will you continue the journey, or will you give up? Will you continue to believe and hope and pursue love and joy, or will you give in to despair?

And then, as you consider your options in this moment of reflection, you hear a few people approaching. You recognize them as compassionate friends who love you and get you, and they have dropped everything just to be with you. I tell you, that's a game changer.

> Compassionate friends have dropped everything just to be with you. I tell you, that's a game changer.

That's exactly what Job's three friends did. They didn't wait for Job to reach out to them. Rather, they took the initiative to saddle up and go to him. As they approached him, they made sure he knew how much they "got it," weeping aloud when they laid eyes on him. And then they simply joined their broken friend, sitting with him in silence on a pile of the ashes of his life.

Of course, I don't really want people to wail out loud over my desperate circumstances. That would be embarrassing and pretty awkward. But to have people around you who care so deeply about you that their emotions overwhelm them? We all need that.

John, Nicole, Ryan, and Megan have been those friends for us, and we for them. They worried about us and prayed with us in 2005 when we thought two of our children were going to be uprooted from our care and moved to Virginia to live with an aunt they'd never met. They cried with us in 2011 when we miscarried the only pregnancy we'd ever had. They stood by us (literally) in 2014 when our oldest son was placed under arrest for violence and escorted from our house in handcuffs. (Nicole even sustained some injuries from that ordeal.)

With friends like this, you can overcome any obstacle.

Our friends can't solve all our problems, though we covet their wisdom. Their greatest impact has come through the understanding, the subtle head nod, the whisper of "I know." Those things have brought abundant healing. One of the main themes in this book is that we experience the greatest healing when we discover we're not alone. Having friends like these on this journey with us has brought that healing.

> We experience the greatest healing when we discover we're not alone.

We are often asked, "How do you find people like this?" We'll talk about that in chapter 10.

Never Meant to Walk Alone

I believe the only hope in this world is found in knowing and following Jesus. It's found in choosing to lay down your life before Him and allowing Him to lead you through the darkness and wreckage. As I look back over just the past few years, I can see His hand in our lives. Our path has been far from rosy. In fact, the word I'd use is messy. We've made four trips to residential treatment facilities for one of our kids, we've become grandparents in our midthirties, some of our kids have had run-ins with law enforcement, we almost lost one our kids to suicide, and we've had to start from scratch financially after I was terminated from a well-paying occupation in the church.

Yes, our journey has been far from perfect. Rather, the past four years have been desperate, dark, defeating, and seemingly hopeless. But Jesus has never let go of us, not even when we felt as if we'd never survive or never overcome. I couldn't imagine walking through these struggles without His mercy, grace, and providence. He's provided for us—not in abundance, mind you, but often in proportion to our need at the time (although my flesh sometimes still confuses my wants and my needs).

> One of the biggest ways we've experienced God's grace is through community.

One of the biggest ways we've experienced God's grace is through community. We've realized how true and real God's design for us is. We were never meant to walk through this life alone. We were never meant to try to live out the faith journey on our own. Throughout the Bible it's clear—God brought people into one another's lives so they wouldn't be alone. Moses had Aaron and Hur. David had Jonathan. Jesus had 12 disciples who walked with Him for three years. (Side note—they not only walked with Him but were homeless with Him too! That's commitment.)

When everything fell apart on Job and his life became a pile of rubble, his three friends showed up, cried out on his behalf, tore their robes, and then sat with him in the rubble for seven days, saying nothing. The faith journey is not meant to be lived alone, and the same is true for the foster care and adoption journey. Never on this journey were you supposed to be isolated and lonely. You've undoubtedly felt that way before, but that's not the plan for you or your life.

Oftentimes the way to find hope in Jesus, the way for that hope to become real and tangible, is to connect with others. I believe He brings others into your life to reveal His love for you. To reveal hope to you. That's how hope becomes real. It takes on flesh and blood.

Your friends may simply sit with you in the rubble of your life, quietly saying nothing. You and I need people who understand us and care about us so much that they're willing to drop everything to come to our side.

> We need friends who love us so fiercely, they feel the deep emotion we feel.

We need friends who love us so fiercely, they feel the deep emotion we feel. They feel the loss we feel over the child who left our care and returned to their birth family. They ache with us over our longing for our daughter to give us, her parents, a real hug instead of giving her affection to strangers. They grieve over our child's impulsivity, which has led to suspensions at school and visits from the police.

I'll never forget the day John and Nicole found out their oldest daughter had mitochondrial disease—a terminal disease that makes people unable to fight off illness. Kristin and I cried with them as they explained how she probably wouldn't live to be more than ten or eleven years old. We still cry with them today. And they cry with us over our son's diagnosis of a fetal alcohol spectrum disorder (FASD). They've cried with us over another child's depression. Together we cry.

There's power in being together, isn't there? Think about it. Just saying the word "together" fills you up and gives you hope. You suddenly feel invigorated, alive, and ready to tackle anything that comes your way. When we are *together*, the most isolating, defeating, heartsick feeling can be washed away like a sand castle in high tide.

Me Too!

My friend Andrew (whom I mentioned in chapter 3) and his wife, Michele, founded the annual Refresh Conference just outside of Seattle, Washington. As far as we're concerned, Refresh is the best conference in the country for foster and adoptive parents (and they're not paying me to say that!). When Kristin and I walked into our very first Refresh Conference a few years back, we looked at each other, exhaled, allowed our shoulders to relax, and whispered, "We're with people who get it...and get us!" They understood our struggles without us even uttering a word. Their intentionality toward the broken, bleeding hearts of foster and adoptive parents was like healing ointment in very deep wounds.

During the 2016 conference, they passed out auctioneer paddles with the words "Me Too" on them in bold white lettering. Then during each main session, they shared real-life stories from real-life foster and adoptive parents. They invited the audience to raise their Me Too paddles anytime they heard something they personally identified with. To see this unfold was healing in the deepest parts of our wounded souls.

- I've been investigated by Child Protective Services three times. (Me Too!)

- I am parenting a child who routinely acts out, hurts me, and hurts his siblings. (Me Too!)

- I started this journey hopeful, but now I feel defeated and ready to give up. (Me Too!)

- I love my child, but sometimes I regret adopting her. (Me Too!)
- My son suffers from a FASD, and it has almost taken the life out of me. (Me Too!)
- My child is in residential treatment and I don't feel guilty. Our life is peaceful. (Me Too!)
- I feel so tired from this journey, I don't know how I'll face another day. (Me Too!)

Over and over, hundreds of paddles were lifted in unison, proclaiming parents' identification with the broken words of another. We felt as if we had carried a 1000-pound yoke around our necks into the place, but it was removed, piece by piece, as each paddle went up.

One of the most amazing sights was watching people walk across the aisles of the auditorium to connect with other parents who raised their paddles at the same time. What a transformational experience. Not only did that person muster up the guts to honestly say, "Yeah, I struggle with that too," but then they found another flesh-and-blood human being who had the same wound. And that's precisely where we begin to find hope. Sometimes Jesus becomes the most tangible to us when we meet other human beings who raise their hands over the same struggle that we have. This doesn't necessarily solve the issue, but it does tell us one thing—other parents feel, limp, and hurt the same way we do.

> "I've been there, man. I know how that feels. I'm on my way."

The Scriptures don't spell this out, but I'd like to think that Job's friends heard about his woes and immediately thought, "I've been there, man. I know how that feels. I'm on my way." As fellow human beings, his friends had experienced some form of loss, some form of devastation, or some form of hopelessness in their own lives. Surely they had experienced the pain of rejection, the agony of defeat, or the suffering of deep loss. I'm willing to bet that sometime shortly after learning about their friend, they each thought, "Me too." Whatever it was, it prompted them to do something very powerful—they traveled far to be with their friend.

That's what we all need.

A Few Resources

We often travel to conferences that provide powerful "Me Too" experiences. Here are a few of our favorites.

- The Refresh Conference Chicago (refreshchicago.net)
- The Refresh Conference Seattle (therefreshconference .org)
- Christian Alliance for Orphans Summit (cafo.org)
- Rejuvenate Retreat (foreverhomes.org)
- Road Trip for foster and adoptive dads (roadtripdads .com)

Am I an Awful Person for Thinking...?

"Sometimes I just wish she would go away and never return. I have visions of a case worker showing up and saying they've found a different home for her. Then they take her, and I don't feel sad. I feel like an evil person for thinking that!"

Perhaps you've had similar thoughts that you wouldn't

share with anyone because they are so dark, so unbeliev-able. Are you an awful person for thinking thoughts like this? No, you're not, and here's why.

1. *You're human.* And like every other human, you're imperfect. No one can play his best game every time he steps on the court. The important thing is, when you stumble, you reach out for help and regain your footing.

2. *The challenges are great.* We live in a fallen world, filled with darkness, and the adoptive and foster care journey is no exception. You've entered your child's difficult world, and though you sometimes wish you could back out, you don't. You choose to love instead.

3. *You're exhausted.* This journey takes every ounce of your energy and then some. Exhaustion can lead you to think and sometimes do irrational stuff. But there's an answer to your struggle...

You're not alone.

Isolation is a breeding ground for your darkest thoughts. But when you find someone you can trust, someone who has probably had similar thoughts, someone who will love and accept you regardless of what you say, try sharing one or two of those thoughts and watch what happens. The condemnation, the sense of failure, the shame...they're all washed away in the pool of shared experience.

No, you're not an awful person for thinking those thoughts. Rather, you are the person God asked to enter your kids' dark world and love them. And you said yes.

5

I Didn't Sign Up for This

Learning to Accept Your New Normal

Let me begin by saying this to you...I know. I've been there. I've walked in your shoes. No one told you about the way trauma rears its ugly head. No one told you about the real story behind his bed wetting, her rage, his impulsiveness. You jumped into this journey with two passionate feet and a heart to bring light into the darkness of a broken child's life. Now you're exhausted, and your kid is holding your entire family hostage.

Believe me, I know. I've crawled through the same trench you're in. I know the regret you sometimes feel for choosing adoption. I also know the shame you feel over that regret. I know the grief you go through because the ideal life you dreamed about is slipping through your fingers. The children you brought into your home with such love and adoration have pushed every boundary and made choices that cause those around you to raise their eyebrows.

You've tried to draw your kids close and love them unconditionally, but they continually push you away and pursue relationships that are toxic and superficial.

So you whisper, "I didn't sign up for this." And that has you wondering…is there any hope?

Where Is the Hope?

This journey can turn out different from the one you expected. You often find yourself isolated, alone, defeated. We get it. In the past, even people in the church—people we might expect to accept us for who we are, brokenness and all—have turned their backs on us. The nursery director told us they couldn't handle our son because he cried too much. *Cried* because he was traumatized. *Cried* because he was scared. *Cried* because he had been in two foster placements prior to living with us, and the trauma went deeper than a cavern.

It leaves you feeling hopeless. And then there's that thought again…"I didn't sign up for this." More hopelessness. More despair. So, where is the hope?

Signed Up

The truth is, you and I *are* signed up. This is our new normal. Our children have come from trauma so dark, we can't imagine it, let alone understand it.

My child has permanent brain damage. Nothing will ever change that. He will always need assistance in some fashion. He will always struggle through life. It's reality. You may struggle to form a genuine bond with your child for a very long time. This is the reality, my friend.

So now we have a choice. We can shake our fists at the heavens and say, "This wasn't part of the deal," or we can choose to move forward, love our children through the trials, work to understand trauma, and live to the best of our ability in this new normal.

I can't go back in time and undo what has been done. I can't go back and fix my child's broken past. I can't go back and safeguard our family for what was to come. If I could, I would. However, I *can* love my children for who they are now and strive to look past their behaviors to the heart that beats inside of them. I've found that when I stop dwelling on what I wish would have been, and accept what actually is, I find hope quicker.

> When I stop dwelling on what I wish would have been and accept what actually is, I find hope.

I'm sharing this with you for one reason: We need to be real. There's hope in the real. It's important to stop and get real about some of the things you are feeling right now. Yes, we do need to reach out for others, and yes, hearing or seeing someone else say "me too" is transformational and healing. But what about the deep, dark feelings or thoughts that spin around in your head? What about those awful thoughts you've had toward your child or your family recently? What about the feelings of regret or the deep denial you've been wrestling with?

Yes, I know these exist in you because they exist in me too. Maybe you're wondering how to overcome those. Maybe you're searching for a way through them. As healing as camaraderie is, you still have to live with the reality of your circumstances. You still have to wake up each day and deal with your child's trauma, which manifests itself in really out-of-control behavior. As nice as it is to hear someone say, "I know," or "Me too, I've been there," you're not released from the constant spin cycle of your daughter's attachment disorder or violent disposition. So now is the time to be honest and open.

Stop right now, put this book down, pull out your journal (if that's your thing) or a blank sheet of paper, and write out some of the thoughts or feelings you've had over the past several months or years of your foster or adoption journey. It's okay, you can be honest. Make sure no one is watching you. Take as long as you need. I'll wait.

So, I'm going to assume you took some time to write a bunch of stuff down. Maybe some things you've said to your children or spouse recently that you're not proud of. Perhaps some thoughts that have been bouncing around in your mind lately, and you feel ashamed that you're thinking them. Can I just say this? *It's okay.* As you've heard me say already, you're not alone.

Be honest...it feels kind of good to get them out, right? Maybe you still wince a little when you lay eyes on what you wrote, but there's a bit of freedom coursing through you. That's what honesty does to you. Saying or writing some of the thoughts you've been thinking about this whole journey doesn't necessarily give you a solution or an escape route. But it releases you from the pressure you've been under to keep holding tightly and privately to the things inside you.

> There isn't a week that goes by when the thought, "I didn't sign up for this," doesn't flash through my mind.

There isn't a week that goes by when the thought, "I didn't sign up for this," doesn't flash through my mind. We've been through the ringer with one of our sons. Because of his fetal alcohol spectrum disorder, his brain is in a constant state of simmer. He's always a hairpin trigger away from exploding. More times than I can count, he's blown up over the smallest things, and that sometimes results in an all-day tantrum (often at the expense of our other family members). He's even harmed some of our other children, destroyed personal belongings in our home, and had the police show up a time or two. It's been embarrassing, exhausting, and defeating—so much so that I can barely describe the experience in words.

I love our son more than anything. In fact, I believe deeply that he has hope and a future. I believe that God has a special plan for him. It's very hard to see right now, but one thing I know to be true: I cannot determine my child's future based on his 13-year-old behavior. Why? Because as we saw at the end of chapter 3 (and will discuss further in chapter 13), God created every human being on this earth with purpose. All 7 billion of us. Whether we choose to live within that purpose and plan is up to us.

This is true for my child. In my most desperate moments with him, I've gone to the darkest places possible in my mind. There's nothing you've thought that I haven't. I totally understand. This is one of the primary reasons we founded our blog, *Confessions of an Adoptive Parent*, and I wrote this book. We want you to know you're not alone. Sometimes you feel isolated on this journey, as if you're the only person who thinks the way you do, reacts the way you do, says the things you say, or loses your cool the way you do. You're not. On the other side of these pages sits a person who is broken just like you.

Hope in the Mountains

In the fall of 2016, three fellow adoptive fathers and I launched the very first retreat exclusively for foster and adoptive dads in the mountains of Colorado. It was called Road Trip: Colorado. Its purpose was to create a safe space where dads just like us could share their wounds, fears, deepest hurts, and struggles without apprehension or feeling any ounce of judgment. We made it clear from the beginning that this was not designed to be an informational conference. We'd all been to enough of those to know we needed something different.

The four of us planning the event met in Austin, Texas, in May and put the components together. It wasn't long before we had the framework in place. Road Trip was to be a conversation, an experience like no other. But we had no idea how God would use our feeble plans.

From the moment guys started showing up on the first day (70 of them, in all), we knew something special was about to happen. And boy oh boy, did it. For the next few days we stood back and watched the Holy Spirit move. When we felt the need to control things, He seemed to put both hands on our chests and say, "No! Don't screw this up. Keep giving Me space to do what I'm doing." So we stepped aside. Best move we could have made.

We watched men (who are supposedly known for being closed up and unemotional) pour their hearts out. They shared their mistakes as foster and adoptive dads. Their fears on this journey. Their biggest failures. Their greatest hopes and goals. It was beyond anything we could have planned for or imagined.

> How do we find hope when everything seems hopeless?

On the second afternoon we were up in the mountains, I gathered with a group of 40 or so guys for a conversation on finding hope. We were asking, how do we find hope when everything seems hopeless? A hot-topic button for foster and adoptive dads for sure. For an hour we sat together and listened to one another's stories. One guy shared that his daughter, who suffers from severe attachment issues after bouncing around from foster home to foster home, wants nothing to do with him, will never hug him, and rejects any attempt he's made to connect with her. His words still ring in my ear: "I'm losing hope altogether that things will ever change with her. It's hard not to let bitterness replace my affection for her."

Another guy shared how his son, whom he and his wife adopted at birth, has walked away from their home and their faith upon turning 18. When he was little, they thought he was bonded completely to them, but he suddenly changed. The effects of his traumatic past reemerged, and suddenly he was gone.

One by one, the guys around the circle shared hopeless, defeating realities from their lives. Big tears welled up in some eyes like giant raindrops on the edge of a downspout. We hadn't really planned on these intentional gatherings being that big of a deal or even being well attended. We were in the beautiful mountains of Colorado after all, and this was during free time, when the guys could go off and hike, fly fish, or take a nap. But here we were, with 40 out of 70 guys gathered. They were searching for hope. They were searching for answers. As I scanned the circle, I saw the same look in all of their faces. It was as if they were all asking the same thing with their silent expressions: "How do I find hope when everything seems hopeless?"

In the next chapter, we're going to learn how to find hope in an unlikely place. But before we do, let me say this. I understand the trench you find yourself in at times. Kristin and I are often in it too. We frequently find ourselves covered in muck and mire, just like you. We understand every tear that drips from your eyes. We know how deeply you love these precious children you've been given to lead and love. We also know how deeply you wish you could snatch the trauma right out of them. And we know that in no way do you wish you didn't have the children you have. We know full well each ache you feel in the depth of your soul over your child. Never forget, you are not alone!

For those moments when you find yourself whispering, "I didn't sign up for this," here are two very practical things you can do.

1. *Press into community.* We realized several years ago that we couldn't do this on our own. In 2009, when our family skyrocketed from four children to eight, we raised a flag of surrender. We surrounded ourselves with people who understood this journey and loved us unconditionally. We often press into our relationship with those people when we are feeling overwhelmed and exhausted. When you find yourself in this predicament, take some time to press into your support community. Learn from them, lean on them, and let them pour into you.

2. *Accept your new normal.* If we're not careful, those weak moments when we utter the words, "I didn't sign up for this" can cause us to wish for a life void of the painful moments we often experience on this journey. We could each go back in our minds to a day before we had children, when we envisioned life and parenthood turning out a certain way. I know this because I've faced this at times when our journey has been rocky. We could become fixated on the fact that we may not have signed up for this, or we could recognize that we *are* signed up for this and learn how to move forward in our new normal. When I choose to accept the fact that I'm signed up and accept my new normal, I experience an abundance of peace.

Understanding Trauma Changes Everything

Our son crouched next to the claw-foot bathtub in our upstairs bathroom. He was trying to push the tub over with his head. Tears soaked his cheeks. He was out of control and violent. Meltdowns like this had become a daily ordeal. The tantrums sometimes lasted for hours.

I was exhausted and angry. I felt like throwing him outside just to show him that this kind of behavior was unacceptable. I also wanted to show him who was boss. I was not going to allow him to continue dictating the course of our day.

But as I stood in the bathroom staring at him in a ball on the floor, moaning like an injured animal, another thought crossed my mind—"He's afraid." Slowly, my anger was overtaken by compassion. I gently closed the bathroom door, moved closer to my son, knelt down, placed my hand on his shoulder, and whispered, "I know you're afraid, buddy. I know there's something deep inside of you causing you to act this way, and it's not your fault."

In order to help my son, I had to step out of my own experience and remember where he was coming from.

1. *A place of fear.* I grew up never needing to be afraid my parents would hit me (though I did receive a few well-intentioned and well-deserved spankings for misbehavior). I was never starving, nor was I afraid someone would charge into my bedroom, yank me out of my bed, and beat me. I never feared losing our house or ending up in a shelter somewhere. I never watched my mom take

a beating from her drug dealer or the guy she was living with.

2. *A place of abuse.* My mom never used cocaine or marijuana when she was pregnant with me. She took care of herself. When I was a child, my dad never slapped me or punched me in the back of the head for walking too slow, and he never beat up my mom. Our son experienced and saw many of these things.

3. *A place of uncertainty.* Home is what brings us security as children. But for a child who's been removed and placed in foster care, confidence and security blow away like a leaf in the wind. This uncertainty is a wound he carries for a long time. Moved from home to home so many times, why should he risk getting attached?

We don't tolerate our son's out-of-control behavior, but we have learned to love him through his fear. That night in our bathroom, I held our son close for an hour. He tried to push me away, but I stayed until he calmed down, found peace, and was able to interact with me calmly, without heightened emotion, aggression, or defense. Sometimes we've waited through this storm for hours. Sometimes it's shorter. But we've learned to wait through it regardless of the length. For the past decade, we have been a work in progress as we've learned the value of waiting *patiently* through these storms. That night, on the floor of our upstairs bathroom with our son, I realized that I needed to step out of my world and step into his. I chose to stop fighting *against* him and start fighting *for* him.

The Middle of the Wreckage

Discovering Hope Where You Least Expect It

For years I tried to escape the reality of our journey. I wasn't out of touch or in denial over our circumstances. I was very much tuned in to our son's disorder, our daughter's depression, and some of our other kids' attachment or anxiety issues. I just kept wishing for a new day. Deep within me I believed that if we could just make it through our present circumstance, we'd find a place of peace, rest, and hope.

This wasn't just something I dreamed about or thought about; it was something I was consumed by. All around me I would see traditional parents or even fellow foster or adoptive parents who seemed to have everything going their way. From the outside looking in, it appeared as though their children were behaving nicely, the special needs they contended with were not that much of a factor, and they could just be...well, normal.

A few of our friends had adopted years before us. Their children were well-adjusted (or so it seemed), and they appeared to be enjoying the good life. I often found myself jealous, envious, or even bitter. How I longed to get past our present circumstances with our children. How I longed for the days when we could just be normal people for once. People who didn't have to arrange special child care with only licensed foster parents. People who didn't have to stay close to home when they went on a date—or went on a date at all from time to time. (What a novel idea!) People who didn't have to constantly tweak their world to make up for their children's violent, aggressive behavior.

The more I thought about what we didn't have, the more I longed for what I thought I needed. Something better. A new day when all of my problems would wash away and I could just be normal.

My entire perspective changed one day when I met up for lunch with a fellow adoptive dad. He was someone I often envied because he appeared to have a perfect life. As we ate our overpriced sandwich and soup, he began to open up about his struggles with his oldest daughter, whom he and his wife adopted from another country. He shared that she often defied their rules and expectations—but much worse than a "normal child," as he put it. She would become cold and closed off, not speaking to them for days, even trying to hurt them emotionally and spiritually. Beyond that, she had become increasingly aggressive as a teenager. She would often fly into fits of rage and destroy belongings in their home. As he shared, teardrops swelled in the bottoms of his eyes.

> Once I accept the fact that my life may never look "normal," I can get busy finding beauty right where I am.

I listened. I felt for him. I completely understood where he was coming from. As we walked out of the restaurant, he said something to me I'll never forget. "Thanks for stepping into my life wreckage with me, Mike."

Wow, was I humbled! I walked away from our time together realizing two very powerful truths.

* My sense of worth or success cannot be based on what I don't know about someone else. The fact is, all my envy, jealously, and bitterness grew out of my lack of knowledge of my friend's life. Once I learned about his real story, my negative feelings toward him drained away, and I was filled with compassion.

* I may not be able to escape the wreckage of life, so I must learn to live in the middle of it. Once I accept the fact that my life may never look "normal," I can get busy finding beauty right where I am.

Learning to Live in the Middle of the Wreckage

Back to Job's interesting life circumstance for a moment. By the end of chapter 2, Job has faced his first and second tests. He has remained faithful, but his life is a pile of rubble. Literally. He's actually sitting on the ashes of his house, scraping sores off his body. (It's a pretty gross scene.)

We've seen that when his friends showed up, they sat in silence for seven days with their broken friend. Notice where they sat with him—right there in the ashes. They entered into the wreckage of his disastrous circumstance, and there they sat. In silence.

Their broken friend had no idea whether his circumstances would change anytime soon. Think for a moment about how hopeless Job must have felt. He's literally sitting on top of the rubble of his life. His house, his kids, his livelihood, his possessions...all gone. He probably thought, "There's no way I'm getting out of this."

In May 2011, a massive tornado leveled the city of Joplin, Missouri. Several "before and after" YouTube videos depicted the devastation and destruction. Some of the people who lived through it were left feeling hopeless. Others probably experienced some denial as the severity of their circumstances became apparent. Perhaps some thought, "How in the world could this happen?" Maybe others questioned God.

Regardless of their thoughts or reactions or feelings, the residents of Joplin faced a choice—would they choose to live in denial or despair or confusion, or would they learn to live in the middle of the wreckage?

Job faced the same choice. The Scriptures say his friends sat down with him—not at a distance from him, not outside of the destruction, but *in* the devastation of his life. And Job himself was at a crossroad—he could give up, blame God, and die (as his wife suggested), or he could learn to live in the wreckage. He could continue on his journey with God—not *in spite of* his circumstances, but *in the middle* of them—and trust that God was not letting go of him.

> We can learn to live in the middle of the wreckage. We can learn how to find hope, joy, and beauty right there in the ashes of our lives.

We have the same choice on this foster or adoption journey. When everything falls apart on us, we can deny what's happening, we can give in to bitterness and despair, we can give up on today and hope for a better someday...or we can learn to discover life in the middle of our circumstances. We can learn how to find hope, joy, and beauty right there in the ashes of our lives.

If you follow our blog or listen to our podcast, you often hear us openly share about many of the trials we have experienced. One of the biggest is the personal struggle we've gone through with our son who suffers from fetal alcohol spectrum disorder. It's been very difficult because of the pain he's inflicted on us and because of the secondary trauma our other children have endured. In fact, a court ordered him to live in a residential treatment facility for the time being.

Even though he has put our other children in harm's way in the past, they are sad that their big brother can't live at home. The situation may sound hopeless, but I have to tell you—we are not without hope. In fact, we have never experienced more hope and joy. Not because he's away from home, but because he's receiving the help he needs. Our other children are healing emotionally and spiritually. We're presently watching the beautiful process of grace unfolding before our eyes.

Our children aren't angry with our oldest son, and neither are we. Instead of anger, we are filled with anticipation for the future. This expectancy may not be fulfilled tomorrow, the next day, this year, or two years from now. It may be a long, drawn-out journey—a roller coaster of joy, sorrow, hopefulness, and hopelessness over and over again.

I want to remind you of something I mentioned in chapter 1. This journey is far from perfect—in fact, it's extremely messy. It can leave us exhausted and dismayed day after day. But there's immense beauty in this mess. It's in the mess that we sense our need for a Savior. If our lives were perfect, we wouldn't need Him. And without the mess, you and I would never know our children. The dark moments in our children's lives have led them to us. Without the mess, we wouldn't have the privilege of parenting the children we are parenting.

The struggle with this, of course, is our continual longing for a new day, a different circumstance, better behavior from our kids, or a different life. This clouds our vision of the beauty that exists now, and we lose hope. That was my struggle for years. I kept thinking that if we could just make it to a certain place in our lives, or if our kids could just get past this season or that issue, or if we could just be like so-and-so and have so-in-so's life, then we would arrive at a place of peace. We could find hope, and life would be good.

But every time I banked on this outcome, I wound up disappointed or even more frustrated than I was before. My problem was that I kept trying to live outside the reality of our life. I pursued hope outside of the wreckage of our life. I missed the opportunity to live in joy in the middle of it.

Now, you may be thinking, "That sounds contradictory, Mike. How in the world can you find hope, joy, and peace in the middle of everything you're going through?"

I understand where this question comes from. Believe me, many parents have asked me this question, and I've asked it myself.

> We must not get so fixated on tomorrow that we neglect the opportunity to trust Him in the middle of our wreckage today.

But where in the Bible does God promise that we'll have joy, peace, hope, and refuge *after* we get through our trials? After we escape the wreckage of our current circumstance? After our kids grow out of their trauma?

I'll let you in on a little secret—it's not in there. God never promises us that we'll escape the wreckage or that an abundance of peace, and hope, and joy awaits us if we do. Here are two reasons why.

- *Life is a spin cycle of trials, tribulations, and setbacks.* Once we get through one life trial (if we do), another awaits. And another after that, and another after that. That's just the way life goes—especially on the foster and adoptive parenting journey.

• *God has invited us to trust Him in the middle of the wreckage.* If hope, joy, peace, and refuge don't arrive until we get through the storm tomorrow, why would we need to trust God today? Why would we need to hope? Why would we need to invite Him to sit with us in the ashes of our lives? Of course, we do trust Him to lead us to new life and a new tomorrow. But we must not get so fixated on tomorrow that we neglect the opportunity to trust Him in the middle of our wreckage today.

An Invitation to Trust

Job did have a meltdown moment, and his tantrum was a doozy. He questioned God—yes, God! In his little fit, Job challenged the maker of the heavens and the earth. Wow!

In Job 30, he's finally had enough of this wreckage. Sitting on the rubble pile of his entire life, scraping nasty sores off his arms and legs, and listening to others (particularly his wife's advice to give up) is all he can take. So he lashes out at God. He starts to recount how awesome he used to be at following God. How much he did for God. And he questions why God is not answering his plea.

> I cry to you, O God, but you don't answer.
>> I stand before you, but you don't even look.
> You have become cruel toward me.
>> You use your power to persecute me.
> You throw me into the whirlwind
>> and destroy me in the storm.
> And I know you are sending me to my death—
>> the destination of all who live (Job 30:20-23 NLT).

Job questions and questions and questions. His friends had blamed him, and now he is blaming God.

God, meanwhile, just stands by.

Everybody loves a good fairy-tale ending. We enjoy movies and books about heroes who face incredible challenges but emerge victorious in the end. And in real life, we cling to the delusion that God will answer all our prayers the way we want them answered. And so at this point in the book of Job, we're likely to think, "Okay, God, enough is enough. This is just cruel. The poor guy has a point. What has he ever done to deserve this? Can we maybe get him out of this wreckage and let him get on with life as he used to know it?" We're ready for God to appear, to sit next to our broken and ailing Job, to place His arm around Job's shoulder, and to explain what has happened and how Job can get out of it.

But that's not what happens. In Job 38, this is how God responds.

> Who is this that questions my wisdom
>   with such ignorant words?
> Brace yourself like a man,
>   because I have some questions for you,
>   and you must answer them.
> Where were you when I laid the foundations of the
>   earth?
>   Tell me, if you know so much.
> Who determined its dimensions
>   and stretched out the surveying line?
> What supports its foundations,
>   and who laid its cornerstone
> as the morning stars sang together
>   and all the angels shouted for joy? (Job 38:2-7 NLT).

God goes on to ask Job unanswerable questions about earth

and sea, death and life, light and darkness, the weather and constellations...

And it doesn't end with chapter 38. God continues for another entire chapter before allowing Job a brief response (filled with utter humility) at the beginning of chapter 40. But then, God continues on for the rest of the chapter and then some. On and on and on, citing the good and perfect and wondrous things He's done that Job had no part of.

Many readers have questioned God's goodness over His response to Job in the middle of his distress, claiming it's proof that God isn't good or that He doesn't care about the circumstances of human beings. But too often the story of Job is told the wrong way, or the most important aspect of this story is never highlighted.

God's response to Job in chapters 38–41 is not uncaring or cold. Quite the opposite. Instead of giving Job all the answers to his problems, God invites him into a trusting relationship with Him. Paraphrase: "Job, I'm not going to tell you why this is happening; I'm just going to invite you trust Me in the middle of it."

> Instead of giving Job all the answers to his problems, God invites him into a trusting relationship with Him.

And that's the same invitation God has for us on this wearisome and sometimes overwhelming journey of foster care and adoption. As you care for children who have suffered extreme trauma, as you deal with the painful reality of children who were born broken, when you are so tired you just want to quit...God is inviting you to trust Him. He's not likely to answer your questions or even your prayers the way you want them to be answered. He's going to continually invite.

You may make it out of the wreckage (just as Job did at the end of the book), but you may not. You may have to learn how to live in the middle of it and how to trust a loving heavenly Father who never leaves you or forsakes you.

But How Can I Trust When...

You may be thinking, "You don't know my life. You don't know what we've been through with the foster care system. You don't know the battles I fight every day with my children."

Well, believe it or not, I do. Trust me on that. I wouldn't write a book called *Confessions of an Adoptive Parent* if I didn't know your struggle. I'm right there in the trench with you.

> Jesus willingly enters the wreckage of your life and sits with you, mourning.

I promise you, Jesus willingly enters the wreckage of your life and sits with you, mourning. He's not afraid to share in the mess of your journey. He loves you and your precious kiddos more than you can imagine. He's not only with you—He's for you. And just as Job's three friends showed up in his darkest hour, Jesus sends people into the wreckage of your journey at just the right time. That's one of the greatest ways the hope found only in Jesus becomes tangible to us in our deepest need.

In the next chapter, we're going to talk about one of the most hope-filled, healing realizations we can come to on this journey:

You are not alone!

How Can I Help My Extended Family Understand My Desire to Adopt?

Most people simply don't understand adoption, and this confusion often results in unpleasant offhand remarks, well-meaning but clueless words, and even rude statements.

A grocery-store clerk asks intrusive questions about your daughter's past. A pediatrician rambles on about the medical history of your son's "real" mom and dad. But even worse are the disrespectful comments from members of your own extended family. How can you respond?

1. *Be kind.* Remember that most folks just don't understand adoption or foster care. And though their words may sting, their intent is to look out for you. They love you, so give them the benefit of the doubt. Keep your first few conversations cordial, listening even when they say things that burn you up inside.

2. *Invite questions.* In private (not in front of your kids!), get it all out in the open by allowing open questioning. Spend adequate time dialoguing with them and learning their perspective and why they say the things they say.

3. *Provide answers.* After you've spent adequate time allowing them to ask you open questions, take the opportunity to provide helpful answers. Share with them your heart for adoption or foster care. Affirm the infinite value of the children in your home. Do not give too many details of your children's story.

4. *Cast a new vision.* Point them toward a positive viewpoint of adoption and foster care. Explain that you are leading these children into the wonderful future God has for them. Affirm that your decision to adopt or foster is yours, not theirs, and that they

can respect your decision without understanding or agreeing with it.

5. *Define boundaries.* Be honest about the pain their words have caused, and clarify what language is and is not acceptable moving forward. Extend grace as you describe future conversations.

6. *Enforce consequences.* "As far as it depends on you, live at peace with everyone" (Romans 12:18). Work for peace, but if others aren't willing, you may have to distance yourself and your family from them, at least for now.

You Are Not Alone

The Healing Power of
Shared Experience

By the time the spring of 2012 arrived, we were so desperate we were ready to quit...on *everything*. Marriage, parenting, friendships, church, living in a neighborhood, even life itself (seriously, there were days). Our son with a FASD was pushing us to the edge and beyond. A year earlier, he had spent four months in residential treatment for extreme behavior. His violent outbursts, impulsive choices, and continual aggression toward his siblings had made him too dangerous to stay in our home.

Since we had adopted from the foster care system in Indiana, where we live, we were invited to take part in a special group designed to help families like ours create permanency and attachment with our children. It sounded like a good idea, but in the condition our family was in, we just didn't want to do anything else, let alone attend yet another meeting.

Besides, this was a support group of sorts. Both of us hated support groups back then. We had endured many bad experiences with them in the years previous. We faced our fair share of judgment from small groups in our church or adoption groups. We didn't need another person criticizing us or our parenting, and we certainly didn't need to show up at a place with our out-of-control child, just to be told how much we were failing as parents!

The answer was just about a flat out *no* until Kristin read the email with details on the group. They were offering free food and free childcare! Considering our dire circumstances, we decided that was a win-win (even if it was only for a few hours). So we made the 25-minute drive down to Indianapolis, where the group was meeting. As we drove, our son called us every name in the book, aggravated our other children, and continually threw items at us in the car. Several times I almost turned the car around and went back home.

When we arrived, we ate our free food, checked our children into their childcare, and proceeded up to a small room with a very large conference table in the middle of it. One by one, eight other couples came in and took their seats around this table. No one looked at anyone, and no one said a word. The looks on their faces were much the same as ours, and I realized they didn't want to be there any more than we did. (Note to anyone who leads a support group: Offer free food and free childcare, and adoptive and foster parents will show up—guaranteed.)

After a few minutes, a dark-haired woman in her early thirties walked into the room, greeted everyone, and took her seat at the end of the conference table. She smiled as she looked around the room and told everyone who she was. "Here we go," I thought to myself. "She's probably going to 'teach' us how not to be awful parents. Does she even understand what it's like to parent a child like mine? Does she have any clue?"

I folded my arms and fixed my gaze on the table before me. I had already made up my mind about this so-called support group. It was the last place I wanted to be. I thought no one in this entire world went through what we were going through with our children. No one understood why we adopted in the first place, and no one knew the storms we were facing at that moment.

I felt so isolated and so did my wife. We continually beat ourselves up, thinking, "Am I the only person who thinks like this? Am I an awful person for wanting our out-of-control child to go away or stop talking? Did we make a mistake in adopting him?" These thoughts constantly weighed us down.

The facilitator opened the meeting by suggesting, "Why don't we go around the table and share our stories of how we got here, what we deal with, and what we hope to get out of this group. We'll start here on my right."

The family to her right began. Five years earlier, they had adopted an eight-year-old girl from the foster care system. She was from a dark situation, and their hearts broke for her. They knew they had to do something to help, so they became licensed foster parents and took her in. Once the birth-parents' rights were terminated, this couple made it official by adopting her and giving her their last name. It was a joyous day for all.

But just a few short years later, she began stealing and lying. Then she graduated to sneaking out and getting picked up by the police. Now she was a full-blown addict to both drugs and sex. Every attempt to get her to follow house rules, stop stealing, and stop sneaking out was futile. She was every bit of the word "defiant."

The next family rolled up their sleeves and showed the group their actual scars from their child's violent meltdowns, which usually resulted in someone bleeding or something being smashed. The woman sharing had to pause frequently to get through her sobs.

The next family shared how hard it's been to form a bond with their daughter, who continually pushes them away and chases after strangers.

On and on and on, couple after couple, each sharing their deepest wounds, regrets, fears, and struggles. It was as if every person in the room rolled up their sleeves and revealed the scars of their journey...openly and honestly, with vulnerability and transparency.

Every now and then I glanced over to see what the facilitator of our group was doing. As each couple shared, she simply nodded with a look of compassion across her face. Occasionally she would say quietly, "I know...that's hard stuff...I'm so sorry you're going through that...hang in there...you're not alone."

"You're not alone." Those words pierced my heart and buried themselves deep into my soul.

"You're not alone." Those words pierced my heart and buried themselves deep into my soul. At the end of the night, we picked up our kids and made the 25-minute drive back home to Northside Indianapolis, where we lived. Our kids fell quiet as our van hummed along the highway. I looked over at Kristin, who was riding quietly and looking out the window ahead.

"Why was that so powerful?" I asked.

"I don't know, but I feel the same way," she replied.

"I feel alive," I continued. "I can't wait to go back. And to think I really didn't want to go."

That night I realized that incredible healing power is available when you find out you're not alone. In fact, just discovering there are others on the journey who hurt like you, fear like you, long for hope just like you...this speaks light into the darkness of your soul.

It forges hope where there's hopelessness. It brings life where's there's death or decay. We all need hope. We all need to know we're not alone.

Like us, you probably began this journey with a full heart, ready to love children unconditionally, regardless of the circumstance. And while that heartbeat still exists, you've quickly realized how hard this journey is. You may have had the wind knocked out of you. As soon as you began taking in foster care placements, you realized how messed up the foster care system can be. You have dealt with rude case managers. You've stood before judges who say they have the children's best interest in mind but give birth families another chance, even though the time for termination has passed. Maybe you spent your every dime to get to China or South Korea to adopt, but once you arrived home with your brand-new baby, you discovered the attachment issues they developed while living in an orphanage. And now you feel helpless to stop them from placing constant stress on you and your other children.

Listen to me: You are *not* alone. As you grieve, hurt, regret, feel the deepest pain, and mourn the difficulties of this journey, I see you. More importantly, I get you, and I'm with you. I don't speak or write to you as one who's made it out of the trench, but one who's currently in the trench. I'm covered in the same muck and mire you are. I have the same hopes, fears, dreams, apprehensions, and passions you have.

And most importantly, Jesus is right there with you too. He knows exactly what you are going through. His heart breaks for your children when your heart breaks for them. He understands the isolation you often feel because no one seems to understand what you're going through. He knows what it means to do the right thing and be rejected anyway.

I'll say it again...you are not alone! I know how passionate you were when you first entered this journey. I know the love that beats within your heart. I know you love your children deeply, just as we love ours. But I know how complicated and wearisome this journey can be. I know that in the midst of loving the children you've been called to lead, you've found the life almost completely stolen from you at times. You are not alone.

This book and our Confessions community have two goals: First, we want sit with you in the middle of the wreckage of life, just as Job's friends initially sat with him. Second, we want to show you the hope we've found. It's in Jesus and those who have chosen to follow Him.

This isn't a churchy, cheesy response to your pain and suffering. You may have been really beaten up by this journey. You love your kids, yes, but you feel defeated by the special needs you're parenting through and the trauma that manifests itself daily through outbursts, rage, and more. We know the last thing you need is a Hallmark card or a saying from a Christian bookstore placard. You need something that's real, raw, and authentic. As we move into part 2 of this book, which is about finding hope, I want you to know a few things.

> I feel safer knowing that I'm not alone.

We're in the water with you. We're not standing on the shoreline. We're not shouting "Jump!" as we stand on a sandy beach. We're calling to you as we bob in the waves. And now that you're in, we're treading next to you, saying, "This journey is good, it's awesome, and it's what you're called to do. Trust me. But there will be times when defeat and exhaustion set in like a dust storm. When that happens, know this: There is hope—you're not alone!"

We're raising our hands. As I mentioned before, when we attend a Refresh Conference and see parents raising their Me Too paddles, we feel as if our load just got a little lighter. It never fails. Every time I see those paddles go up, I feel encouraged, and I choke up a little. I feel safer knowing that I'm not alone. That there will never be enough craziness pouring out of me to make these people walk away. I feel reassured, but more than that, I experience healing. I want you to know that same healing. We are not only in the water next to you—we're raising our hands with you and declaring, "Me too!"

We have limps and wounds like yours. There's not a scar on your body or on your heart that we wouldn't understand. Many of ours probably look a lot like yours. This is a difficult journey. It's filled with unimaginable light and beauty, but it's also demanding. It's hard to parent children through major attachment issues. It's hard to stay positive when your child rages and traumatizes the rest of your family. It's hard to contend with judgmental remarks from neighbors or emails from teachers who think you're the problem. I know exactly how this feels. I have the same limp you do. I know the wounds you've sustained all too well.

Choosing a Support Group

These days we have become big believers in support groups. Sure, we had our distaste for them early on in our journey because we had experienced a few bad ones, but we have found a lot of hope through our connection to other people. In fact, we have been working closely with our friends at Chosen and Dearly Loved and also at Replanted Ministry to help them launch a national initiative called Me Too Groups, which helps connect foster and adoptive parents into support groups all across the United States.*

I will leave you with a few key characteristics to look for when you are considering joining a support group (like the group I

---

* For more information, visit their website at www.metoogroups.com.

described earlier in the chapter). I'm basing these characteristics on two things—the example we saw in Job's three friends in Job 2, and our own experience over the past several years. Here are five big things you need to look for in genuine support community.

1. *People who willingly enter the wreckage of your life circumstance.* Much like Job's friends, who traveled a long distance, mourned with him, and sat with him in the middle of the rubble of his life (literally) for seven days, you want people who wouldn't think twice before stepping right into the mess with you.

2. *People who are silent when you're broken.* Sometimes the best thing a person can say is nothing at all. No fancy Christian sayings they picked up at a bookstore or Bible study, no Scripture (although there is a time and place for this later), no overused sayings...nothing. Job's friends made a key realization: "They saw how great his suffering was" (Job 2:13). They recognized that there were simply no words they could say to make the current reality of his situation any different in that moment.

3. *People who are in the trenches.* We've found that the best supporters in this world are people who are also foster and adoptive parents. Not always, but most of the time. There's just something about being in the same trench. You see things the same way. You hear things the same. You feel things the same. And you can speak into the mess in a unique way that others sometimes cannot.

4. *People who take timely action.* I mentioned a moment ago that there is a time and place to say and do

something more than just silence. There is a time to take action on your friends' behalf and invite them to do the same for you. You want to be in community with people who know when the time is right to speak, give words of affirmation, make a meal and bring it over, or for heaven's sake, take your kiddos to the park for a bit while you get some sleep, catch up on laundry, or take a shower without being disturbed.

5. *People who point.* No, not point at you! No one needs that, do they? What I mean is, people who willingly enter the mess, grieve with you, know when to take timely action, then point you in a healthy direction spiritually, emotionally, and mentally. We can absolutely lose all control of our emotions in front of our close friends and they'll listen, empathize, and even grieve. But when the time is right, they'll always point us to a better way of thinking and living, and we can do the same for them.

I hope by now you've discovered how not alone you really are on this journey. Discovering this truth can bring healing beyond what you can imagine. In the following chapters we're going to talk about how hope shows up in your life and on this journey. You'll discover how real hope is—even in the middle of the storms or the wreckage of the life you dreamed of.

Part 2

Finding Hope

In this world you will have trouble.
But take heart! I have overcome the world.

JESUS (JOHN 16:33)

8

The Story of Your Scars

Redefining Failure

I know.

I know what you're thinking right now.

You have what I like to call the "Yeah, but" syndrome. Don't worry, we all get it from time to time. It's highly contagious, especially in the foster and adoptive parenting community. We often experience the "Yeah, but" syndrome when we are in tough circumstances and we hear words of hope.

We may be at a conference or a seminar that covers a topic we've struggled with. The presenter gives a new strategy for overcoming the struggle, and as we try to apply it to our lives, we think, "Yeah, but you don't know how badly I struggle with this!" Perhaps our therapist tries to give us a new perspective, but we immediately retreat to "Yeah, but I'm never going to be any better than this." On the foster and adoptive journey, we read books, listen to podcasts, and read blogs that offer words of hope, affirmation, and new direction, and we immediately conclude, "Yeah, but my circumstances aren't changing anytime soon. My out-of-control kid's dark disorder isn't going away. Our chaotic and traumatized family will never get past this."

I get it. I've suffered from the "Yeah, but" syndrome many, many times in the past decade. Satan loves to see us give in to the "Yeah, but" attacks. And that's what they really are. Adoption and foster care are both good. They're really, really good, in fact. And we are doing lots of good when we enter into this journey. So of course Satan is going to attack us. He's going to whisper lies to us.

Satan attacks our hope. He wants us to be convinced that we will never rise above our present circumstances, our present struggles, our present failures. He also wants us to believe that our kids have no hope and that there is no future for them. If he can get us to give up on them, then he can get us to give up on this journey.

Satan also attacks us through our scars. In fact, this is where the "Yeah, but" syndrome festers more than anything. When we survey our lives, our journeys, and our present circumstances, we see scars. Lots of them. We wear scars on our bodies and in our hearts. We've been scarred by failure, and we've been scarred in battles with our kiddos. We've been scarred by deep loss and by the grief we feel when our kids make terrible choices. And we're scarred by shame when we think we've become awful people as we struggle to keep our heads above water.

> Wounds become scars—constant reminders of past failure. But what if our scars mean something more?

When everything falls apart in our homes, with our kids, or in our lives, we immediately point to the wounds and think, "Failure." Then the wounds become scars—constant reminders of past failure.

But what if our scars mean something more?

When Everything Falls Apart

We often remember exactly where we were, what we were doing, or who we were with when certain life-changing events happened. We remember because in some way, whether good or bad, these are defining moments. Defining moments shape us, grow us, change us, and have the power to make us better human beings in the future.

I remember the moment when I found out I had been accepted into the college I really wanted to attend. I remember the night I walked into my college dorm lobby and saw for the first time the woman who would later become my wife. I remember hearing that our country had been attacked by terrorists on September 11, 2001. I remember learning that I was going to be a father.

And I remember exactly where I was, who I was with, and what I was doing when I found out my family was falling apart.

July 2013

"We'd like to have a word with your daughter."

A knock came to my door. You can imagine my shock as I opened the door to find three people with badges on their belts—police detectives looking for our 21-year-old daughter.

"Good afternoon," one of the detectives said. "Are you Mr. Berry?"

"Yes, that's me."

"We're detectives from the Carmel Police Department. Is this your daughter?" He held up a grainy but recognizable black-and-white photo of our daughter and another person. The picture looked to be a still shot from a security camera.

"Yeah, that looks like her," I said, squinting and leaning in for a closer look.

"Is she home right now? We'd like to have a word with her."

"She left for work already," I replied.

"Do you know when she'll be home?"

"I don't. But may I ask what this is pertaining to?"

"Mr. Berry," one of the men replied, "we understand that parents want to know what is happening with their children, but because she is 21 years old, we cannot disclose the nature of our inquiry."

I understood, but no amount of explanation could remove the pit in my stomach, the knot in my throat, or the embarrassment flooding my mind. As they stepped off of my front porch and made their way back to their car, I glanced around my street to each of my neighbors' houses. "Did they notice?" I wondered. "Did they see three detectives walk up to my house? Did they wonder what I had done wrong?" These thoughts shot through my mind so quickly, I thought my brain was going to explode.

October 2013

"I'm pregnant."

We've never been judgmental people. We understand that everyone makes mistakes. We've made them, and we've always known our children, being human, would make them too. But when we clearly warn our children not to make certain choices and they make them anyway, our understanding is stretched to the limit.

We told our daughter not to live with her boyfriend. We begged her not to sleep with him. She wasn't ready for that kind of responsibility. She had no steady job, no place to live, and no means to provide for a child.

Our words fell on deaf ears.

We couldn't find an ounce of joy as she and her boyfriend sat in our living room and told us they were expecting a child.

Embarrassment set in like an evening tide overtaking a beach. I thought about the impact this would have on our family's reputation. After all, at that time I was serving as the family life pastor at our church. "How will this sit with the congregation?" I wondered. My wife fought back feelings of resentment and shame. "A 35-year-old grandmother! How can I ever face this?" she wondered. I didn't even want to admit that I would be a grandfather at 37.

And then there was the anger. Oh, the anger. We were angry at our daughter for ignoring us, for thinking that we were stupid for trying to convince her that this would be a bad idea. After all, she was already under investigation by the police. She was already in enough trouble as it was. This was the cherry on top of the cake!

January 2014

"I don't want to live anymore."

Tears dripped from my wife's eyes as she listened to our 11-year-old explain that she often laid awake at night convincing herself not to go to the medicine cabinet in our kitchen and take all the pills.

"There are days when I feel like I don't want to live anymore," she explained. "Sometimes I think this world would be better off without me in it." My wife couldn't believe what she was hearing.

This was not our once happy-go-lucky kid. This was not the little girl who played with Barbie dolls and danced in circles through our house, making up her own tune as she went. This was not the creative, imaginative child who had the most beautiful little voice you could imagine.

Now she no longer wanted to live? Now she thought the world would be better off without her? Even as I type those words, my eyes fill with tears. To imagine life without her was (and still is) unimaginable!

We took the news hard for weeks, lying awake at night and wondering what we had done wrong to cause her to arrive at this place. We meticulously combed through every fiber of our parenting to find the missing piece. We worked feverishly to get the bottom of her depression, spending hours on the Internet searching for answers.

March 2014

"It's bad, Mike!"

My wife's words echoed in my ears. It was just after lunchtime on a warm spring day. I remember everything so vividly. The sun was high in the blue sky. Birds were chirping back and forth as they flapped from storefront overhangs to telephone lines nearby. I had just finished meeting a friend for coffee at a local Starbucks when I received a frantic call from Kristin.

Through tears and broken words, she explained that one of our kids had made a choice that would change our lives forever. The specifics are too personal to share here, but the situation was so serious that Kristin had already called the authorities. Investigators were en route to our home, and I needed to get there as soon as possible.

My breath was taken away. My chest constricted, and I felt as though I had a thousand-pound weight hung around my neck. I couldn't speak, couldn't think clearly, and had no idea what we were going to do. I realized later that this was the definition of lost. The situation felt completely hopeless and out of control.

April 2014

"You can't live here until..."

As I've mentioned, our son suffers from a FASD. His brain was permanently damaged when he was in his birth mother's womb. Part of his brain will forever be missing. That reality has been a tough one for me to grasp. I've fought back feelings of rage toward his birth mom over the years. I've had moments when I wanted to grab her, shake her, and demand an answer as to why she would selfishly put her needs above her unborn child!

Our son has a beautiful heart. God gave him one of the most compassionate and kind spirits I've ever seen in a human being. As a younger child, he was always first to run to the rescue of a friend on the playground who was hurt or who was being bullied. As an older elementary kid, he was loyal to his friends, even protecting them in fights. Even now, as a teenager, he is quick to ask how his brothers and sisters are doing. He often tells us of his plans to become a caregiver, just as we were to him when he was still in foster care. When one of us is sad, he's the first to ask if we're okay and what he can do to help us. "If only we could help him be this way consistently," we often say to ourselves.

But the dark side of him is impulsive, aggressive, and often violent. He doesn't mean to be this way. Really, he doesn't. But the part of his brain that's missing is the part that helps him reason through difficult situations. It's the part that says logical things, like "Don't do that. You'll make things worse. You won't get your way if you throw that."

To this day, we don't know what set him off on that spring evening two years ago. Oftentimes, we never know. We just see the results. It could have been a bad day at school. Or a face his younger brother made at him when we weren't looking. Or an answer Kristin gave him—"Not right now, we're about to eat dinner"—or something like that. All we know is that when the dust settled, my wife's best friend, Nicole, was on her way to the ER, our son was leaving our house in a police cruiser, and the rest of our children were sobbing upstairs behind locked bedroom doors. To say that the events of this night were traumatic would be a great understatement.

Our son spent a week in the psychiatric ward of a hospital in our city and eventually was moved into residential treatment—three states away from our home in Indiana.

Just when we thought we couldn't handle another blow to the heart, I received more crushing news.

September 2014
"You're fired."

I served as a full-time youth pastor for 17 years. Sometimes I wondered what it would feel like to be fired. What would I say? What would I think? How would I react? Whom would I call first? Would I flip out, give the person firing me an earful, tell them what I thought of them and how ugly their mother was...or would I just stay quiet and say nothing?

As it worked out, when the person delivered the news on that warm morning, I said nothing. I shook his hand and left the room. I was numb. The salary that fed my family, provided for our medical care, and paid my mortgage was suddenly gone, blown away like a leaf in the wind.

I had no idea what I was going to do.

September 2016

"You're under arrest."

Our son has struggled for the past 13 years, and so has the rest of our family. The word "struggle" is an understatement, but I really have no other word for what our life has been like with him. The damage he's caused in his fits of rage, the stuff he has broken, the personal belongings he has stolen from others…it's too much for me to count up or keep track of.

He returned home after the April 2014 incident and subsequent residential treatment, and he's held our family hostage ever since. If something doesn't go his way, if he doesn't get the answer he wants, or if he believes he's right when others say he's wrong, he flips out. He physically attacks us, and we end up hunkered down in an upstairs bedroom, locked away from his rage.

Since receiving his diagnosis of a FASD, we've spent a decade fighting with him and for him. We believe in our son. We know that he has a future hope and that God has a plan for his life. We believe this more than anything. But we're so tired of the constant battle.

Through those years, we've often told him that if his inappropriate behavior and choices continued, we were likely to lose our power as parents. "Buddy, the police are going to end up intervening, and we won't be able to stop them if they arrest you. You've got to stop doing these things."

We always approach our son with love. We have compassion for his disorder, and we know he didn't cause it. He was the victim of his birth mother's choices. But as we've learned, there's only so much we can do or say. Unfortunately, as I write this, our son is sitting in a cell in juvenile detention.

On September 29, 2016, he flipped out again and physically attacked both of us. The rest of our children were fast asleep in their beds when this happened. We battled with him for nearly an hour before we had no choice but to involve the police. It was a gut-wrenching decision. The officer who responded had been to our house on two prior occasions. This time, there was no question what was going to happen. He placed our son under arrest and drove him away to our local juvenile detention center.

Out of the Ashes

This certainly was not what we pictured when we first got married and started dreaming of raising a family. None of us enter parenthood thinking, "Gosh, I hope this kid makes terrible life decisions when he's older, gets arrested, and goes to jail." You just don't think like that when you're a new parent or when your kid is growing up. Nor do you plan for a series of events like the ones I just shared.

By now, you can probably see pretty clearly why I relate so well to the story of Job. I'm sure what I've already shared has caused you to identify too. As Job sat on the rubble of his home, scraping the rotting flesh off his arms and coughing in the smoldering ashes of his once-perfect life, did he look at everything around him and think, "I've failed. This is all my fault"? We know that he eventually asks God what he did to deserve such treatment. Did he feel like a failure?

When you think about your scars, what comes to mind?

After all, isn't that what happens when we look at our wounds, our scars, our past hurts? When you think about your scars, what comes to mind? A memory of a time your child with attachment issues pushed you away so badly that you actually got in a car in the middle of the night to find her, only to end up sliding off the road in bad weather (true story from one of our friends)? A thought back to the time you couldn't control your child and the police had to step in? The time you had to shield your other kids from flying objects being thrown from your 16-year-old daughter (true story from another friend)?

Now look at your heart. What about the scars there? If you're like us, you have a few (or a few hundred). The grief you've felt as your child suffered from deep depression? The longing for a real hug after all these years from the son you brought home from another country? The verbal and mental abuse you've endured from your child with a FASD?

Now, be honest. When you consider your physical or emotional scars, do they make you feel like a failure? Do you look at them and think...

- "If I were a better parent, I wouldn't have done that."
- "If I had known a little more about trauma before I adopted..."
- "If I had done more research before his out-of-control behavior started, I would have known how to handle him, and maybe my other children wouldn't have experienced so much secondary trauma."

We beat ourselves up over what we think should have been. We look at our scars, and they remind us of failure.

I have a scar on my right knee. It stretches about an inch from my kneecap down. I received it the summer between sixth and seventh grade, more than 25 years ago. Back then, I played Little League baseball. I wasn't the best on the team, but I wasn't half bad either. I remember the moment I received this scar as if it were yesterday.

During a sweaty July game, I stepped off the first base bag and took a lead toward second. The pitcher was a righty, and I had an advantage. I had stolen a base earlier in the game while he still held the ball and had yet to pitch. This time I was going for it all. He wound up, pulled the ball into his dusty Rawlings mitt, kicked his knee up—and I was off and running full bore toward second base.

I saw the shortstop dart toward the back of the bag with his glove extended. No doubt the catcher was off his haunches, whirling the ball in my direction. I could see the bag approaching. I dropped to slide, extending my left leg out and bending my right leg back at the knee. As I hit the dirt, I felt a sharp pain in my right knee. The pain shot up my right side, landing in my shoulder.

My left foot was met with the shortstop's glove with the baseball inside. As the dust whirled around me I heard the umpire's voice—"OUT!" The opposing team's stand went wild.

I stood up and began to limp back to our dugout—the pain in my right knee was getting worse. As I reached our dugout, I felt a warm sensation just below my right knee. My teammate looked at my leg with wide eyes.

"Oh man, Mike," he snapped. "You're bleeding!"

I looked down to see my uniform turning from gray to dark red just below my knee. There was a tear in my pants too.

My coach came over and began to examine my leg. "I think your day is done, Mike," he said calmly. Under my uniform, just through the tear in my pants, a jagged rock had imbedded itself in my knee. I caught it as I slid into second base. The pain was almost too much to bear as one of the coaches and my dad worked to get the rock out of my knee and clean the wound behind the concession stand. I bit my bottom lip as they gingerly rolled up my pant leg and poured cold water over the wound. In the background I could hear the cheers from parents as our team eventually sealed a victory.

To this day, anytime I'm wearing shorts and I see that scar, it reminds me of the day I got thrown out trying to steal second base. It reminds me of failure. It takes me back to having to sit out the rest of the game because of an injury. It serves as a painful reminder of what I didn't accomplish.

Do you want to know something, however? There are a few things I fail to remember every time I see this scar. I fail to remember that I got to play a game I loved. I fail to remember that I had two singles, a double, and a stolen base that day. And most of all, I fail to remember that our team won the game.

> What if our scars tell us a story of hope?

Oftentimes, we look at our scars as reminders of failure. Memories of times when we screwed up or lost control. Signs that we are failures or our children have no hope or future.

But what if our scars tell us something else, something bigger? What if they tell us a story of hope? Maybe we've been looking at our scars in the wrong light. Maybe we've had the wrong perspective on scars, whether on our hearts or on our bodies. Maybe instead of reminding us of past failures, our scars remind us that we're still alive. We lived to tell about it. That moment didn't defeat us. That dark season on the foster and adoptive journey didn't kill us. This disorder or attachment issue may have beaten us down, but we're still fighting for our kid's heart.

At the end of the book of Job, everything he lost is restored—double! But I have to wonder, did he still have scars on his body from those awful boils? The Bible tells us only that he lived to be 140 years old and that he saw his children's children to the fourth generation.

If Job did have scars, what did they say to him? Did they remind him of what he had lost or of God's faithfulness to him? Earlier, when Job finally melted down and questioned God (chapters 30–31), God didn't offer answers, but invited him to trust in the One who carved out the ocean depths and hung the stars in the nighttime sky (Job 38–41). I'd like to think that every time Job looked at his scars, he thought of that. Not the devastation of everything that happened to him early on, but the goodness of a heavenly Father who never left his side and never stopped pursuing him.

> I'd like to think that every time Job looked at his scars, he thought of the goodness of a heavenly Father who never left his side and never stopped pursuing him.

Our scars, whether physical, emotional, or spiritual, could remind us of past failures, hurts, and losses, or they could remind us of better things. We're still alive, our hearts are beating, we get a new start every day, and we have hope here and now and in the future as well.

It's easy for me to dwell on the devastating moments in my life that I mentioned earlier in this chapter. Really, it takes very little effort to let my mind go there. As I type these words, I could release my mind to dwell on the devastation. The loss. The pain. The embarrassment of having the police show up to my house. The grief of parenting a child who once told us she doesn't want to live anymore. The anger at birth parents who made choices that I have to live with.

> That's where I find hope—not in the wreckage of this journey, but the fact that Jesus has willingly entered into our darkest moments and fights with us and for us in the middle of it.

But I choose not to. I choose to think about the opportunity I still have. The do-over I get every single day, thanks to grace. The life I'm privileged to live. That's where I find hope—not in the wreckage of this journey, but in the fact that Jesus has willingly entered into our darkest moments and fights with us and for us in the middle of it.

Again, you may be thinking, "Yeah, but we've been through so much. My child is incarcerated, and he'll be there for a long time." "Yeah, but I'm a single adoptive parent, and I'm completely exhausted. I don't know how I can take much more of this." "Yeah, but my child's birth parents did so many bad things to him before he came to live with me. Now we're paying for their mistakes, and it's not good at all."

Believe me, I know. I really do. I'll say it again...I have had more "Yeah, but" moments than you can think of. And there's not a situation you're going through that would shock me or catch me off guard. I know it's hard to accept the whole "your scars tell a bigger story" deal at face value. I know your circumstances sometimes cloud any view you have of a sunny day. Before we move on to the next chapter, I want to give you three ways to see the bigger story your scars are telling.

> Gratitude goes a long, long way in helping you see your scars in a different light.

Be Grateful for the Little Things

Gratitude goes a long, long way in helping you see your scars in a different light. We all get caught in the trap of wishing we had a better life, different circumstances, a better-paying job, nicer neighbors, a chaos-free life, or maybe even different children. We all have those dark moments when we think to ourselves, "I didn't sign up for this. Can't I just go back to when life was much simpler?" It's not easy to stop and list off the things we *do* have and are grateful for. But try it and see what happens.

I'm thankful for my kids, even though they drive me crazy sometimes. I'm thankful for their creativity. Our son is always coming up with new inventions that amaze me. I'm thankful for their perspective on the world around them. We have intentionally allowed them to be themselves in every area of their lives.

Our oldest son has a gift for photography. Sometimes, late at night, I flip through the pictures on my phone, completely amazed by his artistic eye. I'm thankful for the compassion I see in our sixteen-year-old daughter. Her spaciness can frustrate me until I'm blue in the face, but her beautiful, compassionate heart always overcomes any frustration I have. I'm thankful for Kristin and for the life partnership we have together. I'm thankful I have a roof over my head even though it may not be ideal.

Be grateful for the little things. Gratitude is a game changer.

Be Realistic, but Don't Dwell on Failures

You're talking to the king of dwelling on failures. I still beat myself up for something I did in 1988 when I was 12 years old. I'm not kidding. It's ridiculous, I know. We do this though, don't we? We dwell so much on our failures that we leave little for positive thinking.

> I can look at my scars and be reminded of past failures, or I can look at my scars and be reminded that I'm still alive and there is hope.

I think that in any tough circumstance, we can be real about what's going on but still look at our lives and our scars with a positive perspective. It's a choice. It's your choice. It's my choice. No one can make this choice for us—only we can. I can look at my scars and be reminded of past failures, or I can look at my scars and be reminded that I'm still alive and that there is hope.

In 2016 our son was led away from our home in handcuffs. He was charged with battery in our home and at a summer camp he had attended. He spent three months in juvenile detention. It was devastating. We feared the worst. We had heard stories of the judicial system locking up kids and throwing away the key without ever finding out the real story behind their behavior.

But in an amazing turn of events, the right people at the right time began entering our story. A probation officer, whose job had to do with paperwork and numbers, became an advocate for our son because she saw something special in him. A court-appointed attorney went the extra mile for us, taking a special interest in our family and fighting for our son in the courtroom. A residential treatment facility was staffed with the most caring, dialed-in people you could imagine. These unexpected events brought us hope again and again.

We could spend all our time dwelling on our son's pile of past failures. We could focus on his difficult present circumstances. Or we can open our eyes and see what is unfolding before us—hope. Even when the journey looks bleak and we're faced with circumstances that knock us down, there is still hope...there is still more light than we could have imagined.

Choose to See the Good

This is another choice we have to make. It's easy to allow darkness to permeate our thoughts and vision. We know so many people who just seem to be Debbie Downers. I'm not kidding. The outlook is bleak with their foster children. The courts haven't moved to termination yet, so they're down and out and bummed about everything.

We get it. But we also know that dwelling on this will get you nowhere. We've had many moments, in foster care especially, when things were bleak. One time after we'd been caring for two of our kids for more than two years, a case manager called us and told us that an aunt in Virginia, whom the kids had never met, was thinking about coming to get the kids and take them to Virginia. The kids we'd had in our care for years. The kids we'd poured blood, sweat, and tears into. It was a very dark and desperate time in our foster care journey.

I remember feeling complete anxiety as I considered the possibility. I felt fear. We were so close to finalizing their adoption...and now this.

But that's when my wife looked at me and said something that changed my heart and mind. "We need to stop right now and pray about this. If we don't, it will eat us up inside."

She was right. I was on the brink of letting doubt, disillusion, and desperation dictate my thoughts and feelings. I was choosing to see nothing but the bad in this—so much so that I had forgotten about the good. So we knelt one afternoon in the living room of our house and prayed. It restored good sight to my eyes and my heart.

This takes practice, but you *can* choose to see the good in your journey. It's about your perspective. Yes, your child may have special needs that leave you exhausted, but are you going to dwell on that, or will you fix your eyes on the truth that you get to be her parent? Are you going to dwell on the fact that this journey may not have turned out the way you expected it to, or will you fix your eyes on the fact that you're on a beautiful journey and you're raising children who needed a forever home?

As I write this, it's summer break here in Indiana where we live. The past few days have been filled with visiting the pool and parks, staying up late, and sleeping in. A few times I've found myself standing back and feeling overwhelmed as I watch my family play together. I couldn't have imagined anything more beautiful (even with some really hard moments).

It took me a while to look beyond the hard stuff, but when I finally did, my eyes were opened to the immense beauty surrounding me. Our son's smile. Our daughter's creativity. Our younger son's imagination. They are all incredible gifts that I get to enjoy. I would never see this if I was busy dwelling on the hard moments.

Your scars can remind you of past failures, or they can remind you that you are still alive, there is hope, and your story isn't finished yet. If you're still alive and breathing, there is hope.

Before moving on to the next chapter, try this brief exercise. Take a moment to write down every awful, dark, desperate, and bleak moment you've walked through on the foster and adoptive journey. Be detailed. Write as much or as little as you need to or want to. No one else will read it.

After you've spent some time writing out all of the bleak moments, shift gears. Next to what you've already written, or below it, write out all of the amazing, hopeful, awesome moments of the journey so far. Your list may look something like this.

- *Awful*: We were investigated by Child Protective Services twice.

- *Awesome*: We have been blessed to be able to bring these two boys into our home and give them a forever home.

- *Awful*: My son was diagnosed with a FASD and is impulsive and violent.

- *Awesome*: My son also has a very compassionate spirit, and he is funny. He makes me laugh all the time. I'm so thankful I get to be his mom.

You get the idea. But here's the most important thing I want you to do in this exercise: Write down more awesome things than awful things (remember, we're focusing on the good). And make sure you end your list with something awesome. It's very important you do this. Trust me, you'll be tempted not to end with the positive. You may even get on a roll and before you know it, you've got a whole list of negative, awful dark things. That's okay. It may take you a time or two of doing this before you find more positives than negatives. I totally understand this. It's happened to me before too. But one of the best ways to find hope in your journey is to choose to focus on the hopeful elements in spite of the difficulties you're facing.

> One of the best ways to find hope in your journey is to choose to focus on the hopeful elements in spite of the difficulties you're facing.

Are you ready? Okay, here we go. One...two...three...write!

The Voices in Our Heads

Overcoming Spiritual Attacks

As soon as you wrote down some awesome things in the exercise at the end of chapter 8, I bet you began to hear *the voice*. You know the voice I'm talking about, right?

It never fails to interrupt your otherwise pleasant thoughts. It whispers to you the moment you start to feel good about your circumstances. The moment you taste an ounce of emotional or spiritual freedom. The moment you realize you had a good day with your kid. The moment you experience a win, big or small.

I hope you were able to write down a bunch of awesome things on your sheet...

- "I'm called to do this."
- "I'm *not* a failure."

- "My child is mine, I am his mamma, and nothing will change that."
- Or as Stuart Smalley would say, "Doggone it, people like me!"

You wrote those truths, you put your pen down, you got up, and you felt pretty good inside. Maybe you even felt as if nothing could stand in your way or take you down. Encouragement raced through your veins like adrenaline. You began to see your life, your parenting, and your difficult child in new light.

But later, when you walked past that sheet of paper or it slid out from between the pages of this book, you saw the awful things you wrote before the awesome things. You began to reread them, and before you knew what was happening, you began to relive them in your mind. They embedded themselves in your heart like a worm burrowing into the earth. And even though you had written some awesome, true, valuable, and encouraging things to counter those awful things, the awful things jumped off the page and back into your mind.

And now you can't escape them. You keep hearing them in your mind. Like a voice in the night, they whisper. You're right back where you were before you went through the exercise. You feel defeated. You feel down again, and you're struggling to find a way to get back up.

That, my friend, is exactly what your enemy, Satan, wants to happen. He's planned it that way. More than that, he wants you to believe all the awful things you wrote down. If he can convince you that you're no better than your failure, no better than your shortcomings, no better than your sin, he wins. First Peter 5:8 says, "Stay alert!

> The sun has risen, and you're still alive. And because you're alive, there is hope.

Watch out for your great enemy, the devil. He prowls around like a roaring lion, looking for someone to devour" (NLT).

He's like a big, quiet, calculating cat, crouching in the reeds of your life, waiting for you to take one wrong step. Perhaps that step is to bypass all the awesome things you wrote and stare at the awful things for moment. When you do that (and you surely do, just as I do), he begins to whisper. He moves all around you, repeating the challenges you wrote down so loudly in your mind that you stop hearing the awesome things. You forget that while you are parenting a difficult child, you're *this child's* parent—that's your calling from God. You pass by the truth that your family, though not perfect, is together. You barely notice that the sun has risen and you're still alive. And because you're alive, there is hope.

In chapter 8, I mentioned several really terrible things my family and I endured for a span of about four years. That season was devastating, defeating, and discouraging beyond anything I've ever endured. Early one morning, just after facing a DCS investigation and realizing our family was coming apart at the seams, I found myself sitting alone in our living room. All the lights were off, and everyone else was still asleep. I couldn't stop my mind from racing. I was at a loss. I had no idea how we were going to find our way through the pile of rubble we were in.

Get up and fight for your family.

It was then I heard a voice. But it wasn't the condemning the voice of Satan that I wrote about above. I could hear this voice in the echoes of my mind and heart. I recognized it because I had heard it before. Over the previous 25 years of my spiritual journey, I had heard this voice often. It was a soft, a quiet whisper spoken directly to my heart. I've always known the Holy Spirit to be courteous and kind, never forceful or pushy. This time was no different. The whispering voice spoke through the chaos of my broken life and simply said, "Get up and fight for your family."

I would love to write that upon hearing this voice, I rose valiantly and, like William Wallace screaming "Freedom!" in *Braveheart*, summoned my last bit of strength and responded with a resounding "Yes, I will!" I would love to tell you that my eyes lit up and my heart nearly beat out of my chest when the Spirit spoke. But that's not what happened.

As soon as this voice spoke, the voice of the enemy bled through. "Stay down," he said. "Quit. It's not worth it. You're tired, after all. There's nothing you can do to make your circumstances any better than they are. Your kids are lost, and that's not going to change."

And sad to say, I conceded. "I'm tired of getting up and fighting. I'm giving up. I quit."

I ignored the Spirit's voice and listened to the voice of the enemy. Do you see how that works? A spiritual battle is raging over you, your children, and your family. It plays out in the form of competing whispers. The voices may be too quiet for others to hear, but in the spiritual realm, it's a bloodbath. It's a clash of light and dark. It's the mother of all battles. Over you. Over your children. Over your family.

> The Spirit speaks too, but sometimes it's hard to hear His voice through the raging storms of our life.

Unfortunately, because of our present circumstances, we often give in to the voice of darkness. After all, our circumstances are painful, and the enemy knows exactly how to hit us and what to say to us. The Spirit speaks too, but sometimes it's hard to hear His voice through the raging storms of our life.

"Get up and fight," the voice said again. And once again, I hesitated. I closed my eyes tightly and actually started praying *against* the Spirit because I didn't want to hear what He was calling me to do! I even slid off the couch to my knees, as if this super-spiritual position would help me drown out the voice.

"Get up and fight for the heart of your family." The voice continued until it flooded my mind, invaded my heart, and left me feeling as though I couldn't ignore it anymore. Maybe this is how young Samuel felt when he heard the voice of the Lord calling to him in the middle of the night.

Alone in the early morning darkness, I snapped back. "I don't want to fight anymore. I'm tired, I'm defeated, I'm ashamed, I'm lost...I don't want to fight—I want to quit."

I placed my hand over my heart to feel it beat within my chest. It was so fast. It's amazing how arguments with the Lord can do that to you. But in that moment, it wasn't fear that caused my heart to beat faster. It was exhaustion. It was desperation. It was the anxiety of running on empty, living in the red, and having no hope that our circumstances were going to change.

I had nothing left to give. To the core of my being, I was empty. So I said no. In that moment, I couldn't believe our circumstances were ever going to improve. I couldn't believe in hope. The wreckage around me was too much to take. So I stayed down, just as the enemy had hoped I would.

For the next week I worked hard to ignore the Holy Spirit's direction. He kept whispering, but I just kept ignoring. I had conceded that our situation was hopeless and our circumstances could never change. Through that difficult season, my wife and I held on to each other and talked together more than we had in a long time. But we had yet to yield to the voice both of us were hearing. We failed to see anything positive in our lives. Neither of us had the strength to fight. We had faced enormous odds many times in the past, but the current state of our family had cut us to the core.

The enemy takes advantage of strategic opportunities to pounce. One of his tactics is to attack immediately after you experience a major win—with your children, in your family as a whole, or in your personal life. This had happened to me two years earlier.

Bushes Still Burn

In the summer of 2012, I faced a big challenge. I was about to start a new job at a large, well-known church in Northside Indianapolis, where we live. I was to be part of the senior leadership team, helping to make major decisions for the direction of the church. I would also lead the family-ministry team—eleven productive, high-caliber people. I had previously served on teams like this one, but I had never led one. Lots of work, lots of pressure, and lots of demands. I was excited for the new opportunity, but I was terrified. Petrified, to be exact.

On a warm night that August, I lay awake in our bed, staring at the ceiling, overcome with worry and self-doubt. Was this how Moses felt when God told him to return to Egypt? Moses had replied, "Who am I to appear before Pharaoh? Who am I to lead the people of Israel out of Egypt?" (Exodus 3:11 NLT). In the spirit of Moses, I cried out in the darkness, "Who am I to lead this team or help lead this church?" I just didn't think I could do it. The voices in my head were screaming that I wasn't qualified to lead at that level, telling me my past leadership failures disqualified me from this kind of task. Satan was as real and present as ever that night in my room, throwing every lie, regret, and past failure at me that he could.

But then the voice of the Holy Spirit spoke softly: "Mike, I will be with you."

Back to our family in crisis. In the quiet of that early morning, I suddenly realized that those same negative voices I'd heard when I was about to start that new job were speaking to me again, trying to convince me that I couldn't fight. Trying to get me to believe that I would never have the energy to contend for the heart of my family, that my failures as a husband and father were too great, that my family was a hopeless case.

Can I tell you something? Satan will not rest until we are convinced we are hopeless and lost. That's what fuels the very fires of hell. He wants us to believe we are unqualified and unworthy. The way he works is often subtle. He doesn't just come right out and speak to us in his true voice. He's much too sly for that.

In the book *Wild at Heart*, John Eldredge points out that Satan impersonates our own voice and uses it against us. That's why we believe the lies we're hearing. That's why we think they're true. That's why we often turn back from danger, shy away from challenge, or retreat from the battle.

Think about it this way—the Bible says that Satan masquerades as an angel of light. If he were to speak to us in his true voice, he would sound something like one of Tolkien's orcs from Middle-earth, and we'd flee from him. He would be terrifying. But instead, he approaches us with a much more cunning and convincing strategy—he uses a familiar voice. Our own. The one we hear all the time. And not only ours but also the voices of our friends, our family, our coworkers, and even our social media followers. It's how he works. And far too often, it's how we fall for the lie.

> God never calls people to do something because they are qualified. He calls them because they are willing.

But thanks be to God that He, through His Spirit, has the power to speak louder than the voice of the enemy. The truth is that God never calls people to do something because they are qualified. He calls them because they are willing. He calls people who make themselves available to His kingdom call. Burning bushes still exist. He calls to us in the most unlikely manner, during the most unlikely times in our lives—even the dark ones.

When I realized this truth in the middle of our pain and agony, it changed me. So I made a choice. I stopped ignoring the Spirit and started listening. I stopped my ridiculous arrogance and opened up my heart. It wasn't easy at all because my finite mind was telling me, "Stay down. You're too weak to fight."

But I used the last ounce of my strength to ask God to give us His strength. Then I decided to get up and fight. I decided that Satan would not win my family's heart.

Maybe that's where you are at this moment. Maybe, even though you wrote down some amazing things in the exercise at the end of chapter 8, you can't stop looking at the awful things. You're fixated on them. You can't stop obsessing over your mistakes as a mom, your failures as a dad, or your regret as an adoptive parent. You can't stop hearing the voice of the therapist who criticized your parenting. You can't stop hearing the mean gossip you heard from neighbors you thought were your friends. You can't stop replaying the condescending things your child's teacher said to you, or the way that IEP (individualized education program) meeting made you feel about yourself.

Maybe you feel incapable of believing anything better or beautiful about your life and family. That's the strategy of your enemy, Satan. If you're succumbing to this, it's exactly what he had planned, and he couldn't be happier about it. When you think about it, doesn't it make you just a little mad? Satan makes you feel the same way the playground bully makes your child feel at school. You hope and pray that you'll run into the little punk and his parents at the grocery store and get the chance to go a little *Mean Girls* meets Liam Neeson on them. Am I right?

It sure makes me mad. Mostly because I love freedom. I love physical freedom, but I also love emotional and spiritual freedom. I don't want anyone to put restrictions on me as a human being. And that includes my heart and mind. I want to be free.

A few years ago I learned how to overcome the voice of the enemy. It's pretty simple, actually. It has to do with a prayer I pray just about every single day of my life. You can pray it too. Ready? Here's goes...

"Holy Spirit, please speak louder than the voice of the enemy."

That's it. I know, it sounds simple and isn't very wordy. Nor is it fancy. It's just a simple, to-the-point request. It really doesn't need to be complex. Nothing about following Jesus does. We just tend to complicate things because that's what human beings do.

> "Holy Spirit, please speak louder than the voice of the enemy."

Pray that prayer the next time you hear the condemning voice. The next time you see the awful things you wrote down and they begin to drown out the awesome things, pray that prayer. Walk around in a park and pray it. Over and over. Write it on your bathroom mirror. When you wake up in the morning and hear the voice, whisper the prayer. Before you go to bed at night, say it to yourself.

I want to be clear. This is not a one-and-done prayer. The voice of Satan whispers to you every single day of your life. Every time he does, utter this prayer.

It's not a fix-all prayer either. After you utter it, you must believe it.

Your enemy prowls around like a lion, ready to devour you. Remember the way he usually works: He hijacks your voice—the voice you recognize, the voice you've grown up hearing—and uses it against you. That's why you believe it. And he never ever sleeps. He never takes a vacation from trying to get you to believe you're not good enough. That's why you need to continually whisper, "Holy Spirit, please speak louder than the voice of the enemy."

Before you move on to the next chapter, take some time to do this now. Here, let me help.

Finding Perspective

One of the things we teach in our online parenting course, *The Resting Place*, is the great need to take an adult time-out so you can gain some perspective.* When parents put children in time-out, they do so for one reason: to give the child a chance to think about what he or she did to warrant a time-out. An adult time-out is a little different but has some similarities. When you're feeling lost, under attack, hopeless, or defeated, you need to take some time to stop, get away, and think. When it comes to spiritual attacks, this is crucial. Your adult time-out will entail three important facets.

> stop
> be
> listen and pray

Here's what each look like.

Stop. Chances are you've been on a pathway that lends itself to a lot of chaos. Your enemy loves it when life is chaotic. It's perfect opportunity for him to make a move. So then, you need to stop the routine (or lack thereof) you've been living by. Chances are, it's not working. As soon as those children are on the bus, off to summer camp, or with a respite provider, don't move right into your daily tasks. Intentionally carve out time to stop.

Be. Once you've stopped, you need to make time to be in the moment. Get out of the house, go to a park, find a quiet trail to walk on, and soak up the time you have alone. We have a hard time being in the moment, don't we? We are such a society on the go that we have no clue what it means to linger in a moment for a while

---

* Visit our website, www.findtherestingplace.com.

(or how valuable it is for our well-being). Once you've stopped, you need to make time to be.

Listen and pray. This may sound elementary because we often talk about prayer a lot in the Christian community, but never has it been more needed than on this great journey, when we are under attack from a relentless enemy. When you're out on that quiet trail or alone in the park, take time to listen and pray. Go back and forth between the two. Oh, and by the way, turn your cell phone off. Ignore the Facebook or Twitter app while you're taking your time-out.

This may take some time and practice. It certainly has for me. And you can bet that once you take steps to get away in order to hear the Lord, you will feel even more under attack spiritually. That simply means you're moving toward something good.

Limping Together

Building an Effective Support System

I met my friend Mike almost ten years ago when we both worked at a church in Westside Indianapolis. We hit it off almost immediately. We worked in different departments, but we routinely had long talks in the hallways and occasionally met up for coffee or lunch.

Our schedules were busy though. The church we worked in was on the go all the time. His job consumed a lot more time than mine did. I worked with students, and he worked in worship and production. Plus, I had been a parent for a few years by the time he became one. Kristin and I had just begun the journey of understanding FASDs and attachment disorders, so it was safe to say we were exhausted just about all the time.

I remember when Mike found out they were expecting a baby. He was overjoyed but also a bit nervous. We stood in the balcony of the worship center talking. He lamented that he was nervous about becoming a new parent. It didn't help that everyone and their mother wanted to impart their parenting advice to him. Even some who had no children—just an opinion. It was just about all he could take. Many conversations were spent venting about those people. He needed that outlet as much as I did.

I'll never forget sitting down to have coffee with Mike one afternoon. In the weeks that had led up to our meeting, I had dealt with some heavy stuff. Several mistakes I had made, sin that had festered in me, and struggles that I quietly kept to myself. I did so for fear of judgment. I already felt ashamed, embarrassed, and exposed. I didn't need any more raised eyebrows, unsolicited advice, or self-righteous input.

As I sat down with Mike, I didn't plan on sharing any of my personal struggles. We were just enjoying one another's company. But then he began to open up about some struggles he had been going through as a man, a husband, and a father. A few times, his eyes welled up with tears as he shared the details of his failure, which he had never shared with anyone. They just so happened to be some of the very struggles I was facing. I had to smile at one point as he described an incident in his life and the thoughts that followed. His experience sounded just like mine.

> We realized we had the same limp. The same wounds. The same scars. And in this discovery, we found hope.

There we were—two grown men, broken, hurting, stuck in a rut of failure, but definitely not alone. We were broken together. We were stuck together. There's something powerful in realizing this. We discovered that afternoon that we were put together, happy, and okay on the outside, but in our hearts and minds, a battle raged. We realized we had the same limp. The same wounds. The same scars. And in this discovery, we found hope.

Walking away from my time with Mike, I felt the same way I did after the support group meeting in downtown Indy that I mentioned in chapter 8. I didn't walk away with my problems solved or a solution for my sin and failure. Nope. Not even close, actually. My struggles were still my struggles. Mike's struggles were still his struggles. Our words that day didn't release us from the bondage of sin and darkness. Really, only Jesus can do that.

But our words to one another did something equally powerful—they brought hope through the knowledge that we were not alone.

It's like spraining your ankle and hobbling around, feeling sad because of your restricted mobility, and then meeting someone who has the same injury. It's just nice to know there are others out there who are wounded like you. When you make these discoveries, you find strength to face another day.

Job's Three Friends

Back to Job and his three friends for a minute. Job has lost everything—I mean, *everything*—and his friends show up to sit in the ashes with him. They willingly enter into his chaos, and then they set what I believe to be the world's best example for what a person should do when someone you know is grieving deeply. They sat down next to Job and said nothing for seven days! They kept their mouths shut. They didn't share sentimental thoughts, deep truths, or practical explanations. Nothing like that. They just sat with their friend and were sad with him.

It makes me wonder...did any of Job's three friends have a limp like his? Had any of them suffered a deep loss? Had any of them enjoyed a good life until suddenly—*poof!*—it was gone in a cloud of smoke? Maybe the three men traveled a long distance just to sit with their friend because one of them (or all of them) had also suffered terribly. The Scriptures don't say, but I have to wonder.

This account of Job's friends showing up after his life falls apart has become one of my favorite moments in Scripture. It's a snapshot of the kind of people we need surrounding us on this long, sometimes defeating, and wearisome journey of foster care and adoption. Foster care and adoption are both widely known but also widely misunderstood. Most people know someone who has adopted or fostered, or they've seen them portrayed in the movies. But the vast majority of the population has no clue what it's like to be in the trenches.

> What we need most is for someone to sit in the wreckage with us, saying no words, and to simply grieve with us.

They may look at a child who has a FASD and think, "Well, he doesn't look like anything's wrong with him! Why can't the parents control him?" They may know that a girl was adopted from foster care but not understand her attachment disorder, concluding that the adoptive parents simply don't know how to build deep, lasting relationships.

We desperately need people who understand—not so they can give us answers, but so they can come alongside us and sit with us in the wreckage. We need friends who have experienced what we're experiencing. We need others who limp the same way we do.

> We need others who limp the same way we do.

How do you find people like that? We believe in the power of a strong support community. It can be a game changer for families like ours.

Finding People to Sit with You

Recently I was speaking at an adoption and foster care conference about the importance of having a strong support system, and I was using the example of Job's friends in Job 2. As usual, I had someone come up to me after my talk and ask about my illustration. "I loved the example of Job's friends—I'd never read it that way. But I was wondering...didn't his friends end up not being the best supporters in the world?"

We both laughed, and I said, "Yes, actually they did end up like that. Later on, after this beautiful example of friendship and support in a tough time, they pretty much played into Job's sorrow and convinced him to lash out at God." Definitely not the way you would have hoped the story to go.

But Job's three friends began by giving us a great example of support and camaraderie. They provided a perfect illustration of what we need the most when our life is falling apart. We need people who will sit in the wreckage with us. Hope is found there, usually by finding others who love us unconditionally through the mess of this journey.

But as we know, Job's friends didn't continue to be a great example of this. Sometimes on this journey, the friends you start out with aren't the ones who continue on with you. In 2007 we met a couple who seemed to be a great fit for our support system (our inner circle of trusted friends). They were fellow foster and adoptive parents. They were raising children with some of the same disorders and special needs that our kids had. They meshed well with our other friends.

But pretty soon we started to notice a disconnect. They were traveling the same journey we were, but they just didn't see things the way we did. A year or two later, we ended up severing ties with them. Sometimes you begin a friendship with folks you think understand you and this journey, but as you go deeper, you realize you just don't see things the same way.

So how do you go about finding people who get you, who will

support you, and who will never judge you as foster and adoptive parents or as human beings?

Over the years, we've coached hundreds of foster and adoptive parents, logged many hours in seminars and breakout sessions, and recorded hours of interviews answering these very questions. Here are four characteristics to look for when you're establishing your support system on the foster and adoptive journey.

People Who Limp

The most important thing is to surround yourself with people who limp the same way you do. Oftentimes the best support can come from people whose scarred arms or hearts look a lot like yours. They are people who have a dog in the fight, just like you. They have a burning passion in their heart to love children from vulnerable places but have recognized how difficult this journey can be. They understand the daily battle you're in. When your child rages and destroys things in your house, they don't bat an eye because their child does the same thing. In fact, on the way over to your house, he unbuckled himself from his car seat and tried to jump out. These are friends who, much like my friend Mike I told you about earlier, can look at you and say, "I struggle with that. I've failed like that too. I wear the same scars." They share your limp.

People Who Get It

Second, you want people who get it. They are foster and adoptive parents (most likely) who are in the same trench you're in, dealing with the same frustrations you are, and parenting through the same disorders and diagnoses you are. They understand the terminology and the lingo. They are covered in the same muck and mire you are. There's nothing you could tell them that would catch them by surprise.

In fact, much like the other families in the support group meeting I told you about in chapter 8, they don't say a word when you're sharing your heart. They just nod in agreement. They nod because they've felt the depth of despair that you do. They long for hope, just as you do. They are battered and beaten up, but they won't quit because they believe in the children God has placed in their care. And here's one big, important trait when it comes to this point: They have the same hope we do. They understand the wreckage, but they've also found the same hope that you and I have in the middle of it—the healing grace of Jesus.

People Who Are Nonjudgmental

Can I just say this? I hate listening to judgmental people. Seriously, who needs that? No one. Certainly not me and certainly not you. If you've adopted children from difficult places or with major special needs, you know what I'm talking about—the raised eyebrows, the labeling, the accusations, the passive-aggressive comments from professionals who are supposed to help us with our children. We already feel badly about ourselves. We've had our fair share of therapists and pediatricians tell us that we're failing as parents and that our kid would be better off with another family (at least that seems to be what they're saying, even if they don't actually say it). We've heard plenty of people make asinine suggestions ("Maybe you should spank them more often") or ask us if we've read *The Strong-Willed Child*. We don't need to hear someone confirm that we often fail. We already feel this to the core of our being. Bottom line: You and I do not need judgmental people in our inner support circle.

People Who Point

Let me clarify what I mean by this. I'm not talking about people who point at you. We've just affirmed that we don't need judgmental people surrounding us, and people who point at us would fit that category. Rather, I mean that we need people who point us in a healthier direction of living and a healthier way of living.

Our friends John and Nicole, whom I introduced you to earlier in the book, are like a brother and sister to us. They are living exactly the same life as we are (raising children with FASDs and other special needs). They totally get our life because it's their life too. Over the past decade, when Kristin and I have reached our lowest point on this journey, we know we can sit down with John and Nicole and completely lose it in front of them. And they can fall apart with us too.

> At the end of the conversation, we always point one another in a healthy direction for our life and our thought process.

Just recently we all went out for dinner and drinks because...well, we were all about to lose it. John and Nicole don't care if we throw stuff, cuss, or rant and rave. They love us unconditionally and would never judge us. We love them too and would never judge them either. But here's the most important aspect of our friendship with them. At the end of the conversation, rant, or meltdown, John and Nicole do something for us, and we for them. We always point one another in a healthy direction for our life and our thought process. Rarely have we poured out our hearts to each other without sending each other away enriched, encouraged, and challenged.

You and I don't need people in our support system who agree with everything we say. Or who allow us to rant without encouraging us to see things in a different light. Instead, we need people who will join us in our pain and listen patiently, but then, when our rage subsides, turn our shoulders or our eyes in a new direction.

Now, the question that most readers ask after considering that list is, "Okay, I get it. These are the people I need in my inner circle. But how do you find people who fit these characteristics if you don't already know them?" Great question. Rarely have I taught this topic without hearing this question. Here's the short answer.

You interview them.

That's right...you interview them to find out whether they are a good fit for your support system. But what does that look like?

As I mentioned earlier in the book, your greatest support will probably come from fellow foster and adoptive parents on the same journey you are on, but you never know where support will come from. Over the years, we've had some really great cheerleaders come from a small group we were in through our church, or even in the neighborhood. You might find supportive people associated with your kids' school or sports team. Someone at work might be going through a process much like yours. We've met helpful people in many places, but we had to make sure they could be trusted with our deepest, most personal information. So we interviewed them.

"Mike, are you saying we should sit down with prospective people and ask them questions?"

As interesting as that would be, it would also be very awkward. So no, that's not what I mean. This is not an interview like one would conduct when finding a new employee. This is a subtle interview. It's a gradual release of information and then an observation to see how that person handles what you've just told them.

It's much like going into a bookstore, picking up a book you've never read before, and then turning it over to read the back cover. The back cover gives you a 30,000-foot-view of the story line, but it doesn't give you the nitty-gritty details. You may pick up the Cliffs-Notes study guide if you want a little more information. If you're online, you could check out a sample chapter.

So when you "interview" a prospective support group member, you begin by releasing the back cover synopsis of your family's story. Nothing in depth, just the general idea. You may say something like, "We adopted from the foster care system, and some of our children have special needs." It's an overview, but you haven't said what the special needs are or how they manifests themselves on a daily basis with your kiddos.

Then you step back and observe how they process that information. How do they respond? What's their facial expression like? Are they searching for words to say, or are they kind and compassionate?

Depending on how they handle the back cover information, you may release the first chapter. "We have two sons diagnosed with alcohol-related neurodevelopmental disorder. It keeps us on our toes and leaves us exhausted quite often."

And then, depending on your observation of how they handle that information, you may graduate to the full book. "We are defeated regularly. Our child is out of control and often traumatizes our other children. He's been in residential treatment three times, and we're not sure he can continue living in our house on a regular basis." That's the whole deal right there. You don't go to that level unless they pass the first two rounds and you can be sure they are safe to invite into your inner circle.

> Don't go to that level unless they pass the first two rounds and you can be sure they are safe to invite into your inner circle.

A few years back I watched Kristin do this with an acquaintance of ours. We were standing in a cafe in our hometown, waiting to order a pastry and coffee, and this woman walked in behind us. We instantly struck up a conversation with her. She has never been an adoptive or foster mom. In fact, her family usually looks like they stepped out of Pinterest. As we talked, Kristin praised her two daughters for their talent and the beautiful photos we saw often on Instagram.

To our surprise, the woman teared up. Then she began to share some struggles she'd been having with them. As is often the case with teenagers, the pictures never tell the whole story. They struggled with identity and self-esteem like every other kid. Gradually, Kristin shared a bit of our story, but only the back cover synopsis. Nothing too detailed. At the time, our oldest son was still in residential treatment across the country. So when Kristin shared that part of our family's story, she referred to it as a boarding school.

Then we observed her. We watched and listened to see how she handled the information we just gave her. She was very compassionate and understanding. Kristin's conversation with her was a perfect illustration of how to interview someone.

A word of advice when you've just adopted or begun fostering and you're on the lookout for people who understand you and who won't judge. People who belong in your support community will probably not include your family, your neighbors, or most of the people you go to church with. Some of them might fit, but more often than not, that's not the way it works. Here are a few points on what your support community will look like.

This Community Will Be Small

It shouldn't include more than eight or ten people. Picture the normal size of a small group at your church. When I worked in the church, we never put more than ten people into a small group. Once you pass that magic number, intimacy and connectivity seem to lose steam. Of course, if you are already close with six other couples and you have a solid connection with one another, by all means, form that support community. Just don't picture a support community like this as including lots of people.

Roughly ten years ago, Kristin and I formed a strong bond with three other couples. We did everything together. We hung out at each other's houses for barbecues and holidays. We celebrated each other's birthdays. There was a time when we would see each other nearly every week at one of our houses.

It just made sense—we were all on the same journey. We were all adoptive parents, we were all fostering at the time, and we all attended the same church. I remember taking some criticism from a few other couples who were not adoptive or foster parents. They were annoyed that we had formed this bond. It irritated them that we did things together as families and didn't include others in the fun. I think they secretly wanted to be included.

This made sense from their perspective, but it didn't from ours. These folks were skeptical of the adoption process. They had even made offhand remarks to some of us on different occasions. We loved them, but they did not belong in this group of like-minded people. Your community of supporters, your inner circle, should be small rather than large.

> Not everyone will understand the adoption and foster care journey. Most won't.

This Community Will Not Include Everyone

I'll go one step further—it won't include *most* people. Why? Well for starters, as we've already seen, not everyone will understand the adoption and foster care journey. Most won't. It's just not normal for most folks. Even though everyone has heard of foster care and adoption, there's still a disconnect. How I wish it weren't so, but it just is.

Here's one surefire way to know not to include someone in your inner circle: Do they hail you as a hero or a savior for being a foster or adoptive parent? That may sound strange to you, especially if you're just beginning the journey as a foster or adoptive parent. After all, wouldn't you want people around you who love you and lavish love and encouragement on you? You'd think so. But there's a difference between someone encouraging, loving, and supporting you, and someone who gushes all over you, calls you a hero, or constantly refers to you as an angel for choosing to foster or adopt. Let me explain.

In 2002, we adopted our first daughter at birth. She was perfect, beautiful, and ours. After spending a few days off the grid (which wasn't hard to do back then with the absence of smartphones and social media), we finally emerged from our house and took her to church. When we walked in the front door, you would have sworn an A-list celebrity appeared. People swarmed us. A few people even clapped. It was ridiculous to say the least. A few of the older ladies patted us on our shoulders, hugged us, and told us we were angels sent from God to care for this little girl.

A couple who was a little older than us and had kids in elementary school gushed over us and told us how amazing we were for adopting this little girl. "Surely you rescued her out of a tough situation." They asked about her birth family, and we shared what we knew. They asked if her birth mom was on drugs or drinking or had to give her baby up for adoption, and we timidly answered no.

That's when our friend Dawn stepped in. She had been watching the fanfare from a distance. She too was an adoptive mother. Her son, whom they adopted at birth, was an older elementary-aged child.

When the timing was right, Dawn pulled the two of us aside and said, "I want to give you some advice. Your daughter's story is your story and her story to tell—no one else's. Be careful what you share and who you share it with. You never want someone sharing stuff with her that she may or may not have known."

We were suddenly very thankful that Dawn had shared that with us. Our daughter's business, our adoption story, and our family's journey were nobody's business but ours. Dawn went on to tell us to beware of those who hail us as heroes or fall all over us as if we were angels. We learned pretty quickly how right she was. The people who hailed us were usually the quickest to turn on us when they couldn't get past their own confusion about our family. These people were usually kind, but we needed to keep them at arm's distance. Dawn's advice proved to be invaluable for us then, and it still is today, all these years later.

> The people who hailed us were usually the quickest to turn on us when they couldn't get past their own confusion about our family.

Finding Hope Through the Limp

We find hope through the limp. There are at least a few other people—real flesh-and-blood human beings with minds and heartbeats—who struggle the same way you do and have wounds that look a lot like yours. When you meet them, you find hope. The reason is simple—there's power in camaraderie. As I've already said, you may not find answers to your biggest problems, you may not find a solution to your struggle, you may not find a way to help your child through their trauma...but you find strength.

Once again, when you're in the middle of a difficult season on the journey—when you're struggling to parent a child from a traumatic past or who suffers from a disorder that causes certain behaviors—it's easy to feel trapped. It's easy to feel hopeless. But I want you to know that there is hope.

Sometimes you can find hope simply by looking at your life and your circumstances through a different lens or by choosing to look at your circumstances with your children as hopeful rather than hopeless. We have this choice. We can choose which lens we put on as we survey our journey. Even when things are rocky, you and I can choose to see things positively instead of dwelling on the negative. In the next few chapters, we'll build that lens.

You Are Not a Hero

Recently, Kristin shared with me a tragic story about a couple who adopted older children from a foreign country, but after a short period, ended their relationship with them due to behaviors that were out of the couple's control.

My first reaction was frustration. How could they! A disruption only makes the children's trauma worse. But then I realized the couple probably didn't realize what they were getting themselves into. They were following their hearts (which is a good thing), and they had a dream (nothing wrong with that). However, I'm guessing they saw themselves as heroes on a rescue mission.

Both perspectives are dangerous, and both perspectives are wrong.

Children who are adopted are likely to deal with trauma, emotional issues, attachment disorders, or separation anxiety. These may take many, many years and lots of therapy to work through. The loving, stable home you provide is invaluable, but it will not solve these children's problems overnight. The road will be long and difficult, but these two steps will help you persevere.

1. *Enter the adoption journey with the correct perspective.*
   You're not a superhero, and this is not a rescue
   mission. You're a person who's choosing to love
   another person with a difficult background. Do
   this for love and nothing else.

2. *Educate yourself on your child's trauma, attachment
   issues, and disorders.* The child you bring into
   your home is likely to have endured trauma or
   to be suffering from disorders. Plenty of helpful
   information is available at the click of a button.
   Educating yourself will help you establish realistic
   expectations and avoid the pitfall of believing
   you're on a rescue mission.

Behind Every Cloud

Finding Light in Dark Times

I believe in hope. I struggled to find it for many years, but now I deeply believe that this journey is not a lost cause and neither are any of our kids. Sometimes, however, we find ourselves in the middle of such a dark storm that we struggle to see the light beyond.

Recently I was down in Little Rock, Arkansas, at a conference called the Hope Conference. Their premise was—you guessed it— to share hope with weary and worn-out foster and adoptive parents. I was so unbelievably excited to be their keynote speaker for the weekend. I absolutely love doing this. And this organization is doing some amazing things for foster and adoptive parents in the state of Arkansas.

I spent a few weeks before the conference poring over content, praying, and preparing to spend time with the people who would attend. If it was hope they needed, it was hope I would give them.

It's my favorite message to share with foster and adoptive parents because I believe in it so deeply. I don't believe that any circumstance or any journey, no matter how bleak it may seem, is hopeless. The reason is simple—in those bleak moments on our own journey, those difficult seasons with our children, Kristin and I have overcome and found hope. It's real.

The night before my second keynote, I sat alone in my hotel room, unwinding from a very full day and looking forward to day two. I flipped through the stations on my television until I came across the Weather Channel. (I'm a bit of a weather nerd.) The story they were featuring was a reenactment of people stranded on a Texas peninsula during Hurricane Ike in 2008. The people who survived the storm told their harrowing tale while actors reenacted what they had endured.

At one point, one of the survivors described making it through the first part of the hurricane and then everything suddenly settling down. As they were clinging to survival in the attic of their home, his wife looked at him—battered, wet, and exhausted—and said, "Thank God it's over." But knowing what was about to happen, he looked at her and said, "This is the eye of the storm. We still have the back half to go through."

The back half of a hurricane, as the narrator described it, is the most violent and destructive because of all the debris from the front half. That's where the most destruction and loss of life occurs.

As I watched this, I realized that many people on the adoptive and foster journey feel as though they're caught in a storm like this. Tossed about, back and forth, from the front to the eye to the back and then to the front again. You struggle to see how there is any way out of this or any reason to hope at all.

And I get that. Believe me, I do. For the first ten years of our journey, we felt as if we were caught in a storm. We were bounced around between IEP meetings, therapy appointments, difficult visits with birth parents, court hearings that produced nothing new, meltdowns, and exhaustion. We often felt as if there was no way out. People kept telling us to hold on, but we were struggling to keep our heads above water.

Nothing but Storms

Have you ever felt as if your entire journey is one big storm? Have you ever felt like giving up and giving in? Calling your agency, calling the birth mother, and telling them that you're done, that they should come and get the kids? I have.

Most of us probably entered the foster care or adoption process with an ideal. Maybe even a fantasy of how we thought it would be. We dream of walking into an orphanage in Romania and bringing our children into our homes, into better circumstances and a better life. We envision a scared little girl or boy in foster care, and we picture ourselves easing all their fears. We dream of the yet-unborn baby we'll soon meet when the agency matches us with the birth mother.

We make plans. We hope. We dream. We paint a room and deck it out with baby things. We buy blue and pink outfits and make cute adoption announcements from pins we found on Pinterest. We call our friends and tell them of our decision. We browse pictures of children our local foster care agency is trying to place, and with enthusiasm and joy, we send an email to the case manager saying, "I'm in!" With anticipation and nervousness, we wait to meet the little boy they're bringing to our house. We shake his hand and smile. He's expressionless, but we're certain he'll open up soon.

For a while, the journey is good, and you're on cloud nine. "Is this too good to be true?" you wonder. You've heard scary stories about children pushing their parents away, raging because of a dark disorder, and stealing, but you can't imagine that happening in your home. Maybe your child is the exception.

But then you hit a wall, just as I did. Perhaps it's not your children, but your health care providers or school counselors—professionals who are supposed to be helping you and your family. Perhaps your extended family is judgmental and degrading, or they make hurtful comments to your children about being adopted.

Or maybe it *is* your children. The sweet, loving child you brought into your home with love has begun turning into a different person. Maybe you noticed a few signs that were concerning to you, and after having your child tested, you found out he or she does in fact have a FASD. You knew there was a strong possibility they were born drug and alcohol exposed, but now it's documented. The diagnosis has left you devastated.

Or you could be fostering a teenager who pushes every single boundary you establish, attaches herself to negative relationships, or pursues people who are unsafe. You haven't slept a wink in nights. You're filled with worry for her all the time, but she doesn't seem to care.

The person you used to be, the dreams you used to have, your hope for a bright future...they're all gone. All you can see are storms.

It's easy to do this when your circumstances are dire—when you're dealing with tough disorders like FASDs or major attachment issues. It's easy to feel as if your life is nothing but storm clouds when you're wrestling with a foster care system that is backward and inefficient. You've heard me say this already, but I'll say it again—I get it!

> It's easy to feel as if your life is nothing but storm clouds when you're wrestling with a foster care system that is backward and inefficient.

We get emails all the time from people who speak of their circumstances as hopeless, never ending, and never changing. After we give a talk at a foster or adoption retreat or conference, people often walk up to us and say the same thing. Somewhere in their conversation they'll hint at the fact that there's nothing but storm clouds around them. Sometimes the difficulties of this journey can make you feel that way. Sometimes the exhaustion and defeat are too much to take. Sometimes the darkness you're in can keep you from seeing any light at the end of the tunnel.

I'm sure Job had moments like this. He instantly went from having a pretty awesome life—wealth, homes, livestock, acreage, and kids who actually wanted to hang out with one another—to having nothing. And he's contracted a skin disorder that's as gross as the day is long. Surely he too thought, "There's never going to be any hope." Yeah, I think I would feel hopeless too.

When All You Can See Are Ashes

As I write this chapter, the cities of Gatlinburg and Pigeon Forge, Tennessee, have been ravaged by wildfires. More than 250 buildings—cabins, resorts, restaurants, schools, houses—have been damaged or destroyed.

My family was in Gatlinburg for a vacation two years ago. We stayed in a gorgeous three-story cabin overlooking the valley where Gatlinburg is located. That cabin and many others around it are now completely gone. Harrowing online videos show people evacuating with fire on both sides of the roads. I once traveled those roads with my family. I can hardly believe the beautiful place we knew is almost entirely burned.

What is it like for the home owners and business owners? Reports indicate that when the wildfire broke out, wind gusts of more than 80 miles per hour caused it to spread—hurricane-caliber winds in the mountains of Tennessee. The accounts I read also said this happened suddenly, with very little warning. Imagine that for a second. One day you are standing on the deck of your cabin or inside your business enjoying the end of fall and the beginning of the holiday season, and the next day it's all gone. Nothing is left but a pile of ashes.

It's easy to see why people would feel hopeless. When you look at the pictures online, you wonder how the people could possibly rebuild. How will this town of less than 3500, with an economy fueled by the 11 million visitors it receives each year, ever recover?

> It's easy to become so fixated on your present circumstances that all you see are the smoldering piles of ash and the smoke all around you.

It's easy to become so fixated on your present circumstances that all you see are the smoldering piles of ash and the smoke all around you. I'm positive Job felt that way as he looked at his circumstances. I can identify. I have been to some dark places in the past 15 years. I too have looked up and seen nothing but storm clouds. I too have often wondered, "Is there any hope?"

The Sun Is Still Shining

If I told you there was hope in the middle of the storm, would you believe me?

We've already talked about the importance of surrounding ourselves with other people who understand us on this journey. That's one of the biggest ways Jesus becomes real and tangible to us. That's also how He infuses us with hope. When we discover that we are not alone, that others have the same limp, that real-life people just like us wear the same scars and have the same wounds but also have the same passion to love children from vulnerable places, we find hope.

We can also find hope in the middle of the storms of this journey by changing how we look at the storm. By focusing on what we know to be true in spite of the storm.

Think about the most violent thunderstorm you've ever seen. Maybe it was even a big-time storm—a tornado or a hurricane. Picture the storm surge, the high winds, the thunder, the lightning, the debris spinning through air as you peer outside. Hear the sirens blaring and the house shaking every time the wind beats against it. Do you have the chaos in your mind? Now, ponder two things about this storm.

- *It's temporary.* It's not going to last forever. It will pass. Storms always do. There's never been a storm on earth that has continued without end. Even the great flood in Genesis came to an end. Sure, it rained for a long 40 days and 40 nights, and the storm probably felt endless, but it eventually ended and the waters receded. This may be hard to believe in the middle of the storm, but the end will come.

- *The sun still shines behind the clouds.* During every storm, big or small, the sun never goes away. It's still shining. It's just not visible for a time because dark clouds hide it from our view.

> Regardless of how bad your circumstances are, the storm is temporary, and the sun is still shining above the clouds.

Regardless of how bad your circumstances are, how difficult the child you are caring for is, or the hopelessness you feel because of both, the storm is temporary, and the sun is still shining above the clouds. I know it's hard to believe, but it's true. We've endured many long, dark, and violent storms on this journey, and we believe with all our hearts that behind the clouds, the sun is shining, bringing us hope and reminding us that all this pain and agony is temporary.

Kristin and I travel a lot. Rarely a month goes by without one or both of us jumping on a plane to another city somewhere. We love to travel and speak to foster and adoptive parents. It fills us up even though we're completely exhausted afterward. (It's a good exhaustion though.)

Recently, I spoke at a four-day conference in San Diego. It was an amazing conference, and I met some wonderful people. In addition, San Diego is a beautiful city, and while I was there, the weather was nearly perfect. I loved being there and meeting so many wonderful people.

Still, after four days, I was ready to go home. I had left long before sunrise on Father's Day. I missed my wife and my kiddos desperately. I wanted to see and kiss their sweet faces as much as I wanted oxygen.

After nearly missing my flight out of San Diego, I made it safely on my plane and landed three hours later in Denver. When I landed, I immediately knew I was going to be delayed. Massive thunderstorms were rolling in from the west. Before we even reached our gate, the plane was rocking back and forth. Bolts of lightning flashed, and heavy rain pelted the planes and terminal. It was awful. When I reached the departure monitors, every flight had the word "delayed" next to it. My connecting flight home to Indianapolis was supposed to depart at five p.m. but was now pushed back to six thirty. A little time went by, and six thirty became seven—and then eight, and then eight thirty.

This was beginning to look hopeless. I was tired, hungry, and stuck in a packed airport with thousands of other frustrated passengers. I found a seat near my gate in front of the big window overlooking the tarmac. Dark clouds zoomed past the terminal. With each passing minute I became more and more frustrated and wondered if I would ever make it home.

I know...silly, right? Of course I was going to make it home. Never in the history of modern aviation has a passenger been permanently stranded in another city. We all make it home eventually, and this would be no exception. I might have to wait an extra day, but still, homebound I would be. We often think irrational thoughts like this when we're in the middle of desperate circumstances, don't we?

> We often think irrational thoughts when we're in the middle of desperate circumstances.

Finally, after waiting four long hours, I was able to board my plane to Indy. I found a window seat just behind the left wing, still feeling frustrated. Lightning continued to flash, and the wind was still whipping around us. But the tower determined we could take off safely, and 30 minutes later, we taxied to the runway. As we zoomed down the runway, rocking back and forth, I kept my eyes fixed forward, not saying a word to anyone around me and certainly not inviting any conversation.

As our plane left the runway, I suddenly caught a glimmer of a bright light out of the left corner of my eye. I turned toward my window, raised the visor, and caught sight of the most beautiful sunset I had ever seen. Once we bounced through the cloud coverage below, it was smooth sailing. The storm below was now behind us, and we were engulfed in a beautiful sunset. I pulled out my phone and took a picture because I wanted to always remember this sight.

The truth? This beautiful sky was behind that massive storm the entire time. When I was on the ground in the middle of the storm, I couldn't see it. It was temporarily hidden by dark clouds. My situation seemed hopeless at the time, but I just needed to hold on to a truth that never expires—the sun is still shining, even in the most violent storm.

Your circumstance may be dire right now. Your child may be completely out of control, leaving you desperate and defeated. The local foster care system may be yanking you around like a yo-yo every single day. It all may leave you completely hopeless. You may feel as though you'll never find a way out of the storm you're in. But when you least expect it, you will rise above the storm, and there, waiting for you the entire time, will be the most beautiful sunset you've ever seen.

Last night, our second-oldest daughter, her fiancé, and her daughter (our granddaughter) came over for a barbecue at our house. It was a great evening together. We laughed, talked, watched our precious granddaughter play, and enjoyed one another's company. At one point, our daughter and I were standing in our kitchen chatting while she finished preparing a salad. Suddenly I thought, "I'm so proud of this kid! What an amazing, responsible, caring young woman she's become!" I smiled to myself. I couldn't help it.

The journey to this place has been a long and difficult one. From her high school graduation in 2010 until 2013, we were in a storm with her. It felt as if it would never end—the hurricane just kept turning and turning. We prayed and hoped, but the outlook was bleak. But then (as I'll explain later in chapter 13), when we least expected it, the clouds broke, and peace entered the scene. The sun had been shining in the background all along, but we couldn't see it in the middle of the storm.

It was a long journey, but here we are, enjoying a barbecue together. The clouds have moved on, and the sun is shining again.

As you finish this chapter, you may have some heavy feelings spinning in your heart and mind. You may even be wondering how you can look beyond the storm and see the sun. Here are four beliefs that will help you do just that.

1. *Believe in your calling.* You were called to do this. You were called to be a foster or adoptive parent. There's no question. Not everyone in this world can decide to love and care for children from vulnerable places, but you did. It may sound elementary to say this, but I think we often forget about our calling. We lose sight of our original heart behind the journey. There's no question you love your kids. I love mine too. But in the middle of everything we have to do, we forget about our calling. Choose to believe in your calling.

2. *Believe in your influence.* If I told you that you are making a profound impact in your child's life, would you believe me? I say this often in live events I speak at, and it never fails...someone in the audience shakes their head no at me. They simply can't believe that they are making any kind of difference. But you are. We've talked about this truth already in this book, but we need to be reminded. You have no idea how your love and presence are changing the life of your child and changing the future.

3. *Believe in your child.* What about your kids in all of this? What about belief that your child has hope and a future? We'll talk about this more in depth in chapter 13, but I want to encourage you that if you want to see beyond the clouds, believe your child has hope and a future.

4. *Believe in hope.* The hope we have is the sun that's shining beyond the storm clouds. It's ironic that as I type this right now, I'm sitting in the Denver International Airport. My flight is on time and there are no storm clouds in the vicinity. Several years ago, that wasn't the case. I felt hopeless. But the storm didn't last forever. There was hope then, and there is hope now. Regardless of your circumstance with your children. Choose to believe in hope, my friend.

Legends Versus Legacies

Your Influence Goes Deeper
Than You Know

We know the sun continues to shine above the storms raging in your life. That gives you hope for the future when your circumstances are dire. But what about today? You may be able to see rays of light off in the distance, but when you focus closer to home, you may feel as though your efforts with your foster or adopted children aren't making any impact whatsoever. This makes you want to give up. Once again, this is something you are not alone in feeling. We have been there.

Let me ask you a question. Have you ever felt as if the things you say or do for your children are getting nowhere? Nothing you say seems to make an impact. Nothing you do seems to make a difference. No matter how much effort you invest, regardless of the compassion, love, and service you give, your child doesn't seem to be responding.

Are you raising your Me Too paddle right now? Again, you're not alone. We all have moments when we wonder if we're making any difference at all as parents.

> "People who are *legends* have a following. They draw attention to themselves. But those who leave a *legacy* are often faceless—and yet they change many people's lives. If you live as a legend, you'll fade out, and it won't end well. If you leave a legacy, you'll change history."
>
> MARK CHRISTIAN

What Sets You Apart

When I was a youth pastor, I took students every summer to a conference in Michigan called Move. It's an amazing experience and completely intentional for high school students.

One morning as we were sitting in the main session listening to the speaker, Mark Christian, he said something I will never forget. He was talking about making a difference in the world and what real impact looks like. As he helped students compare and contrast worldly success with God's perspective on success, he said this: "People who are *legends* have a following. They draw attention to themselves. But those who leave a *legacy* are often faceless—and yet they change many people's lives. If you live as a legend, you'll fade out, and it won't end well. If you leave a legacy, you'll change history."

I quickly scribbled down this amazing quote. It stuck with me. Later on, I thought about it in terms of what we are called to do. It relates so well to the foster and adoptive journey. How often do we measure our success with our children the same way the world measures success? How often do we evaluate ourselves according to the world's standards? A therapist criticizes us, and we feel like failures.

A teacher is judgmental toward us or our kid, and we want to run and hide because it's too much to take. We take the comments or criticism from people we barely know personally as if they have final say-so over our lives, our parenting, or our journey. Or maybe we are parenting children who are extremely aggressive because of their traumatic past, and we tie their behavior to our identity. This too makes us feel like failures.

Kristin and I know this from personal experience. Our second-oldest daughter made terrible choices for four long years after graduating high school. Even though we adopted her from foster care when she was 17, we felt as if she had always been a part of our family. For years we prayed for her and hoped for good outcomes. But we took the things she did and said to us personally. We doubted that we were making any kind of impact on her life at all. Pretty soon, we felt completely hopeless, as if we would never get through to her.

It was a long, long road for sure. We spent three years praying and praying and praying over her. And for three long years, there were many times when we felt as if God wasn't listening or had abandoned us. And then one night when we least expected it, she came home. Today, many years later, she's grown up, she's healthy, and she's a wonderful mother.

But we've realized something about the foster and adoptive journey—we're not called to be legendary. We're not called to be superstars or even heroes. The difference we make in the lives of our children may not show up or come full circle in our lifetime. But that should never stop us from loving and caring for them deeply. It shouldn't stop us from laying our hearts on the line for them. This is difficult to accept, but the

> Your influence, acts of compassion, and serving heart will make a difference in your child's life. You just might not see it for a long time.

impact we make sometimes goes unseen or unnoticed. You probably already know this. If you're waiting for applause or a big thank-you, you'll be waiting for a long time.

You don't do this for other people's applause or even your children's gratitude. Legends do things for applause or accolades. You, however, are not a legend. You're building a legacy. Your influence, acts of compassion, and serving heart will make a difference in your child's life.

You just might not see it for a long time.

Tricia's Story

I met Tricia when I was preparing for the annual Refresh Conference in Seattle. I was set to interview Tricia onstage as part of the final session on Saturday night. After talking to Tricia, I realized I was hearing a story that was as life-changing for foster and adoptive parents as it was for her.

Tricia had been subjected to ongoing sexual, verbal, and physical abuse from her birth father when she was a teenager. She was like a toy he used and abused whenever he felt like it. Tricia endured this ongoing trauma until she was finally removed and placed in the system. Deeply bitter because of everything she had suffered, she did everything she could to push her foster families away and make them give up.

As a teenager, Tricia bounced around from foster home to foster home. Her routine was simple: Land in a new house with a new family and start defying every boundary they set for her.

Curfew at nine p.m.? "I'll come home at eleven."

No dating? "I'll date whoever I want—and have sex with him too."

No drugs or alcohol? "I'll do as much as I like and reek like liquor when I come home."

No smoking? "I'll light up on the front porch in front of all the neighbors."

Her plan worked. Every time she arrived in a new placement, she immediately started pushing boundaries. She continued pushing until the family finally gave up and called the agency back. Tricia went through six different placements before she aged out.

Her last placement was with an older couple named Ruth and Rich. Tricia didn't know it, but her short time with them would change her life forever. Ruth and Rich were different from the other foster parents she'd known. They were kind, tolerant, and patient. Tricia began her usual game of pushing until the family gave up, but this time it didn't work. And it wasn't for lack of trying.

When Tricia and I were planning our interview, she told me she kicked her routine into high gear when she arrived in Ruth and Rich's house. She went above and beyond to try to get herself kicked out of their house. She would age out soon, and she didn't see the point of staying away from her boyfriend or her other friends. So she routinely snuck out and stayed with them.

Every time Tricia pushed the boundaries with Ruth and Rich, they did nothing...but love her.

Tricia recalls a time she decided to defiantly light up a cigarette in their backyard, which was surrounded by a privacy fence. As she did, Ruth walked out and said, "Oh, honey, you can't smoke back here. Come with me to the front porch, where we have comfortable chairs you can sit on while you smoke."

> "They loved me like Jesus did—in spite of my messy life."

"That was Ruth," Tricia recalls. "Never a mean word spoken. Never a judgmental tone. Always loving, always giving. Ruth and Rich loved me for who I was. They loved me like Jesus did—in spite of my messy life."

Eventually Tricia turned 18 and aged out of the system. At her high school graduation, Ruth and Rich gave her a Bible with money in it. Tricia said, "True to form, I took the money and tossed the Bible. I didn't care about anybody or anything but *me* back then. I left their house in defiance."

Ruth and Rich never gave up on her and never stopped loving her even though Tricia never returned the favor or showed any sign of changing. Perhaps she never would. In fact, some even questioned Ruth and Rich's approach and wondered if their influence would ever make an impact in Tricia's life.

That's what we all wonder when we pour out and pour out with little or no return. We continue to pursue our children even though they push us away and never give us a genuine hug. "Will this ever change?" we wonder. We allow our hearts to be broken over and over by the verbal abuse from our kids who suffer from disorders they didn't choose or cause. We do the same thing again and again, hoping for different results. In the end, some of us conclude, "This is hopeless. She's never going to change." "I'm not making any difference at all. He'll leave and eventually end up in prison."

Here's the hope of a story like Tricia's. When she was 38 years old—20 years after she walked out of Ruth and Rich's home, seemingly never to return again—the Holy Spirit pierced her heart, and she laid down her entire life before Jesus. From there she reconnected with Ruth and Rich and expressed gratitude for everything they'd done for her. Eventually she became a foster and adoptive mother herself.

Do you think Ruth had lingering, hopeless thoughts in the back of her mind? Do you think she wondered if she was really making a difference in Tricia's life? You bet. But she never gave up on her. She never stopped loving her. She and Rich continued to extend grace to her. Eventually, 20 years later, it clicked in Tricia's mind and heart, and her transformation began.

You are making an impact every single day in the lives of your children. It may be hard to see, but that's easier to accept when you remember you're building a legacy!

> You are making an impact every single day in the lives of your children.

The Power of the Dash

The futility of legends and the authentic power of legacies is nowhere more apparent than—of all places—in a graveyard. There you find rows of grave markers. Some old, some not so old, and some brand-new. Each one includes a birth date on the left and the date of death on the right.

And here's the reality: You have no control over the date on the left. You didn't choose when to be born—it was completely out of your control. Your parents decided to make a baby, and you entered the world roughly nine months later. It happened. It is what it is. You may love your life (or not), you may appreciate your parents for making this decision (or not), but your feelings don't change the fact that you were born.

And here's another reality: One day, each of us will stop breathing, our heart will stop beating, and we will close our eyes and die. We will probably not have much control over when or how that happens either. The date on the right side of the marker is pretty much also out of our control. We can't stop it from happening.

Do you want to know what we can control, however?

The dash in the middle of our birth date and death date. Just about every marker has one. The dash represents our legacy. It reminds us of our entire life...

How we loved.

How we served.

How we gave.

Our attitude about life.

Our interactions with strangers.

Whether we were generous with our time, talent, and money.

How we treated those closest to us.

What we did with Jesus.

The way we treated our coworkers and neighbors.

The funny, quirky things we did.

The time we spent with our family (or didn't).

Our character and integrity (or the lack of them).

The moment after you and I take our last breath, that dash will begin to speak. That's the conversation everyone who attends your funeral has in your absence. It's a conversation about you. It's their memories of you. It's the things that drove them crazy about you. Depending on how you lived your life, some of the conversation may be summed up by facial expressions and not words. The dash between your birth date and death date represents your legacy. It's the story of how you lived your life and how you impacted others while you walked this earth.

> You alone can choose how you will live your life.

You can't control your birth year—it happened, so let it go.

And you probably won't be able to control your death year. That's life!

But I've got good news—the dash is completely under your control. You alone can choose how you will live your life. You choose how you will love. You choose what you will do with the time here on earth God has given you.

Very few people may stand up and applaud you for how you choose to live out your dash. You may never receive a medal or an award for the way you loved. But the bottom line is this: You can still choose to make an impact with your dash, even if you never receive any praise for that choice or see the results of it. That's what it means to leave a legacy rather than be a legend.

Of course, many legendary people also left a legacy—Billy Graham, Mother Teresa, Rich Mullins...the list goes on and on. Ruth and Rich chose to use their dash here on earth to build a legacy, expecting nothing in return. They chose to love and extend grace to a broken child who walked through some of the darkest situations. In doing so, they changed her life...20 years after she left their care. They made such an impact on Tricia's life that she is now using her dash to love children from difficult places.

That's a legacy!

Perhaps you're looking at your own journey and wondering if you're making a difference, or even how you can leave a legacy. Honestly, this is not rocket science. In my younger years, I thought that to create a legacy you had to do something extraordinary. "Maybe if I spoke at Catalyst Conference, or was featured on Focus on the Family, my legacy would be made." That may sound strange, but that was my thought process. I misunderstood what created an authentic legacy. It wasn't in the big, dynamic moments (although those may be included). No, it was in the everyday tasks of loving unconditionally and choosing to serve others and put their needs above your own. It's as simple as that. And this is an opportunity we have with our children and our families every single day.

You Can Have a Positive Relationship with Your Child's Birth Parent

Healthy birth family relationships are crucial to success on the foster and adoption journey. We've never allowed ourselves to hold on to grudges or bitterness toward our children's birth parents. We honor them. We've had our moments of frustration and irritations, but we've committed to show them respect, treat them with dignity, and build solid relationships with them. Here are five steps you can take to do the same.

1. *Talk about them in honor.* This was one of the biggest takeaways from our first pre-adoptive parent class nearly 13 years ago. Our kids' birth parents are human beings, and they deserve honor and gratitude.

2. *Never vilify them.* Avoid tarnishing the birth parents' names or causing your children to think of them in a low light. It's easy to allow your frustration to get the best of you, especially when you foster to adopt. But none of us are perfect either. Simply placing ourselves in someone else's shoes will give us a different perspective.

3. *Celebrate their heroics.* When our children have asked us, "Why couldn't my birth mom keep me?" we've responded, "Your birth mom was so brave and so courageous, and she loved you so much, she chose to place you in a situation that would be better for you."

4. *Work to form a solid partnership.* As your kids grow and mature, do everything in your power to form a healthy partnership with their birth parents if that option is available to you. Consider them friends. I just met up with our youngest son's birth father last night for dinner, and it was a great experience. Every time I take our son to meet with him, I walk away encouraged and thankful we met.

5. *Consider them part of your family.* This often catches people off guard. Some birth parents are not suitable or healthy enough to interact with their family. But if your relationship with your children's birth parents is amicable, include them in your family. Spend time with them at a park, or the zoo, or a mall, or a restaurant. Include them in birthday parties or holidays if you can. Don't worry about confusing your children. It only becomes confusing when you make it confusing.

Your kids' birth parents deserve love and grace, just as you and I do. If the tables were turned, we would want the same treatment.

Remember Jeremiah

God Has a Plan for Your Child

I'll be the first to admit—I've had moments on this journey when I've just about given up hope on some of my kids. It's happened three or four times in the past eight years. I hate to admit arriving at that low point. It's not something any parent wants to experience.

It's not that I don't love the kids who have pushed me to this point. I do, with all of my heart. I would lay down my life for any of my children. I love them more than I ever knew was humanly possible. Perhaps that's why I've reached that hopeless point a few times.

I first felt this way in the summer of 2011. It was July. In the middle of what we had hoped would be a fairly good summer break with our kids, we suddenly had to make an extremely difficult decision for our eight-year-old son. His behavior had escalated to a dangerous state. A few months before, he had hurt one of his younger brothers, almost putting him in the hospital. We escaped with a series of stitches, but it was scary and traumatic for us as parents.

That was only the tip of the iceberg. He would routinely terrorize our other children, break things in our house, cuss and scream at us, act impulsively, and disrupt any peaceful interaction we had with our family. We were constantly pulling the car over because he would unbuckle himself and threaten his brothers and sisters.

The day we drove him to a residential treatment facility, I felt hopeless. This was not the picture I had in my mind for our son. I was angry at him, angry with his disorder, and angry at his birth mother for choosing to consume drugs and alcohol. My heart had begun to grow numb toward him because of how exhausted I felt on a daily basis. I was tired of having to walk on eggshells for fear that an eight-year-old would blow up and start to hurt the other members of my family. I was ready for him to go away.

I hated that feeling. "It's not supposed to be this way," I thought to myself. "I signed up to be a parent to him, but I can't keep him or the other members of my family safe—not even my wife." I felt defeated. I felt as though I had failed. On one hand, I was relieved that he was out of my house and that we could experience some peace. But on the other, I felt guilty. I loved him, but I was tired of his antics, his dangerous behavior, and his impulsivity. I reached a point where I couldn't see how there was any hope or future for him.

The second time I had to deal with feelings of hopelessness was in 2012, when my second-oldest daughter was living with a guy who was an abusive alcoholic. We had been going back and forth with her for a few years. She would wise up, leave him, stay with us for a while...and then gradually drift back to him. We saw the writing on the wall, but it took her longer.

We spent three long years praying and praying for that relationship to end. Three years of hoping and begging God to move in her life in a way that only He could. She knew in her heart of hearts that this guy wasn't healthy. We could see it in her eyes, but she felt trapped. Her misguided sense of loyalty drove her back to him time and time again.

I remember sitting in our living room one afternoon staring out at trees waving in the wind and the leaves falling. My eyes landed on a picture on our piano of our beautiful daughter. A surge of hopelessness suddenly flooded my heart and mind. "Will this ever change for her?" I wondered aloud. "Will the chains this guy has wrapped around her heart and mind ever be broken?" I longed to see her free from his grip and his lies. I longed to see her become the young woman she was meant to become.

She didn't look like herself anymore. Years earlier, when she came to us through foster care, she had a sparkle in her eye. When she entered a room, the mood would suddenly become bright and electric. She had a way with people that drew them in and made them feel good about themselves. She was as beautiful on the outside as she was on the inside. To this day, we still laugh about some of the hilarious things she said and did as a teenager. Even though it was late in the game when we made our family her forever family, we loved that kid deeply. The tears we cried over that girl in those three years could fill an ocean.

Tears streamed down both my cheeks as I continued to stare out of the window that afternoon. I prayed, I hoped, I begged...but still I felt hopeless.

A year earlier, I had doubted our son had hope and a future. I had doubted God could ever use him for anything good. Now I was doubting God could ever lead our daughter out of a dark situation. Even though I prayed heavily in those years, I was consumed with doubt. And that's the precise moment my eyes were opened to a powerful truth!

Jeremiah Is Right

I'm not sure when it happened or where I was. I can't remember whether someone said these words to me or I read them directly from the Bible. But at some point, I came across a verse of Scripture that I believe was written to remind foster and adoptive parents that God never makes a mistake. That He has a plan and purpose for every single human being.

In Jeremiah 1:5, the prophet records these words:

Before I formed you in the womb I knew you,
before you were born I set you apart;
I appointed you as a prophet to the nations.

If you're like me—a person who has been around the church for just about his entire adult life—you've heard this verse again and again. For a time, it was on pro-life billboards around the country. When I was a teenager, people in my church wore this verse on their T-shirts at pro-life rallies in downtown Cincinnati. But I never paid much attention to this verse until last year. Our son had just returned home from another stint in residential treatment, and he was once again starting to hold our family hostage with his behavior, attitude, aggression, and choices. That hopeless, lost feeling once again returned to me. But then I thought about this verse, and it suddenly struck me.

God doesn't make mistakes.

God doesn't goof.

No one is an accident.

> Even someone who appears to be completely lost can fit into the story line God is telling about humanity.

Even someone who appears to be completely lost can fit into the story line God is telling about humanity.

Our son was almost aborted. We prayed and prayed that wouldn't happen, and it didn't. God heard those prayers. The birth mother grieved being too late to have an abortion, and she chose to ease her pain with substances. He made it through that too. He was born in 2003 and came to live with us in 2004. Someday, somehow, God is going to use him for something powerful.

In the fall of 2013, our daughter finally decided to end things for good with the guy she had lived with. One night he was intoxicated, and he snapped, dragging her into his house by her hair and beating her up. This proved to be the reality check she needed to see the light and finally end the abusive relationship that had enslaved her for so long. God's amazing story line is beginning to unfold in her life every day since she made that life-changing decision.

We never want to see bad things happen to people, but those bad moments have a way of opening our eyes and our hearts to the reality of life. This reality was a story line that had been on standby in the background of her life all the while. That fateful night when all hell broke loose, she realized she deserved better treatment than she was receiving. She couldn't yet see the future—the responsible, respectful man she would eventually raise a family with or the beautiful child she would bring into the world—but that story was beginning to unfold. We must remember that even when the outlook is bleak and we've prayed till we can't pray another word, there's a purpose and plan for each of our kiddos.

> There's a purpose and plan for each of your kiddos.

Jeremiah was right. He *is* right. There is a purpose and plan for every single human being on this spinning planet. There's a purpose and plan for each of your kiddos. There isn't a situation so bad that God's mercy, providence, and grace can't move and transform a heart.

I realize that you may have a very hard time seeing the light of this truth because of your situation with your kids. You may be dealing with special needs that have pushed you to the brink—or beyond. Your home may be in complete disarray because of the choices your child is making. You may have experienced so much secondary trauma from the outbursts, violence, and aggressive behavior of your children that you can't see how God could ever rectify your situation and use it for anything good.

If this is you, let me offer you some advice. I've been in this hopeless place. I've felt the shame and isolation of our situation with our child. I've come to understand what trauma looks like and how it plays out in our kids' lives. Here are four steps you can take that will help you see your children in a different light.

Remember Their Past

The fact that our children are still alive after what they've come from is a miracle we should celebrate. Maybe your children didn't necessarily come from a dark place, but if they did, praise be to God that they are still alive. Even more so, praise be to God that He saw fit to allow you the opportunity to raise them. Remember, they've come from a traumatic place and an experience you and I may not be able to fully comprehend.

Most of us have never known the deep fear of not getting enough to eat. We can't comprehend the anxiety of having a case manager come to the house we've grown accustomed to and taking us somewhere else. We may not know how awful it is to watch our birth mother or father get beaten or murdered.

> Remember the traumatic past your kids have come from, and you will have renewed compassion for them.

Remember the traumatic past your kids have come from, and you will have renewed compassion for them. When I finally realized our oldest son was constantly in a fight to survive because he was starved as an infant, my heart broke!

Remember Your Own Journey

I don't know about you, but I didn't exactly inspire hope when I was a child. Especially when I was a teenager. If such a category existed, I probably would have been voted "Most likely to fail college and end up homeless." I had to grow up...big-time!

It took a while. I had to walk through the fire of life before I could come out refined on the other side. And just when I thought I had arrived, I needed more refinement, so I had to walk through the fire all over again. I won't ever reach full refinement. Neither will you.

I didn't come from a traumatic situation the way some of my kids did, but I still had to journey to where I am today. Twenty years ago I wasn't able to do what I do today. I wasn't the husband and father I am today. I'm sure twenty years from now, I'll feel the same way.

> Life is a journey for all of us, traumatic past or not.

Life is a journey for all of us, traumatic past or not. And this is never more important to remember than in the foster care and adoption journey. Yes, your son may be displaying some out-of-control behavior right now. But remember, he's come from a place you may know nothing about. Yes, your daughter is pushing you away. But remember, she's constantly in survival mode.

It's not personal, even though it feels that way. You can relate to them in some small way by considering your own growth journey from childhood to today. Remember, you cannot determine your children's future based on their current behavior at eight, nine, or twelve years old.

Trust the Greatest Storyteller of All Time

I hesitated listing this one because it sounds so simple and obvious. But I've found over the years that some of the simplest and most obvious truths can also be the most profound.

I've learned an important lesson about trust—I'm really bad at it sometimes. I can go way down the road of negativity before realizing I'm not placing my trust in the One who carved the ocean depths. I do this often with my kids. Their behavior, choices, attitude, or current struggles can bum me out and leave me feeling hopeless. But God says, "Bring this to Me. Bring all the garbage, devastation, hopelessness, mess, and doubt to Me. I'm not afraid of it. I can handle it."

It's something I often forget. Even as I've worked to get this book finished and off to my publisher on time, I've wrestled with this. I've sent a couple of desperate emails to my publisher filled with worry that I wasn't going to hit the mark or that this material wouldn't resonate with you. And then I realize, "Hold on, I'm trying to do this on my own. I'm relying on my own wits, my own brain, my own talent to get this book done. I'm not trusting God at all."

> You and I need to trust the God who created the universe and gave us life, confident that He holds our broken kids in His mighty hands.

You and I need to trust the God who created the universe and gave us life, confident that He holds our broken kids in His mighty hands. When Job had his freak-out moment and questioned God, God invited him to trust. "No answers, Job...just trust." It's the same invitation God extends to you and me as we work to parent children who've gone through a whole heap of trauma. "Trust me," He invites.

Believe in the Untold Story Line

I love the part of Jeremiah 1:5 where Jeremiah pens, "Before you were born I set you apart; I appointed you as a prophet to the nations." These words contain a lesson that rings true all these centuries later for our precious kiddos: There is an untold story line in the background of their lives. Even though it's hard to see sometimes, God declares to them, "Before you were born, I set you apart. I have an amazing story to tell through your life. I am going to use you for some really awesome stuff someday!"

He certainly did that for Tricia. Remember, there was a time when she would have been considered hopeless. But today, more than 30 years after she walked out of Ruth and Rich's home, God is using her in ways no one would have comprehended when she was a teenager and raising a ruckus.

Our son is not a hopeless case. As I write, he is incarcerated in our county's juvenile detention center. That sounds hopeless. But I hold firm to the words of Jeremiah 1:5. God knew our son before he was born. Before he took his first breath here on earth, he was appointed to communicate God's love to the world. God is going to use him in a powerful (though yet unseen) way. Our son is not without hope. He still has a future. There's still a story that has yet to unfold in his life. I'm convinced of this.

Yes, Kristin and I believe the words of Jeremiah 1:5. We believe that our heavenly Father,

> We choose to remember Jeremiah 1:5 whenever hopelessness begins to creep into our minds.

who is also his heavenly Father, knew him before he was even formed in his birth mother's womb. We choose to remember Jeremiah 1:5 whenever hopelessness begins to creep into our minds.

God has appointed each of us to do great things. That's true for you regardless of your calling in life, and it's also true for your child. You may look at the child you have been called to raise and feel that because of his or her choices, behavior, attitude, and actions, the situation is completely hopeless. But in those moments when you feel that hopeless feeling, let me invite you to do something...

Remember Jeremiah 1:5.

Remember that God knew your children before they were born.

Before your children took their first breath, God knew them. The same God who laid out the blueprint for the universe and spoke all of creation into existence, set your children apart before they were born.

And this God makes no mistakes!

You *Can* Walk into Your Child's School Equipped

"Could you make sure you feed Andre every morning before he comes to school?" our son's resource teacher asked abruptly.

Kristin was dumbfounded. "Andre receives a balanced breakfast every morning."

A moment of silence on the other end. "Well, he comes in to my class every morning claiming that he's hungry and that you don't give him breakfast."

Kristin asked how long this had been going on.

"Well, he's complained about being hungry for the past several weeks," the teacher replied.

"And why didn't you call me?" Kristin asked.

"I've been giving him granola bars and snacks that I keep in my desk drawer, and that seems to satisfy him."

Oh, I'm sure it does, Kristin thought to herself. *And that's precisely why he's telling you he's hungry.* Because of trauma sustained early in his life, our son has major food issues. He could have a huge meal and say he's starving an hour later. We thought we had made this clear to his teacher, but we obviously needed to meet with her.

We were both so angry, we wanted to let her have it. How dare she let this go on for weeks and not call us! We were still fuming when we went to bed. But the next morning, when it came time for the meeting, we decided to change our attitude. Here are five attitudes we've learned to carry to school with us.

1. *We're on the same team.* This is number one. When you walk into a room with a same-team attitude, every conversation is more peaceful.

2. *Crazy never wins.* If you walk into an IEP meeting with guns blazing, belligerent, or rude, your child's needs get lost. The reason is simple. When *crazy* is speaking, people hear and see *crazy.* They don't hear or see the real need!

3. *Collaboration and listening are effective.* As you walk up to the school entrance, remind yourself to keep your ears open, use your words cautiously, and

maintain a goal of creating a better situation for your child.

4. *Be kind but firm.* If you sense that your words are falling on deaf ears, repeat yourself. Restate your position and your requests, but be kind, stay calm, and remain firm.

5. *Include your support team.* We entered the IEP meeting with our support team—our son's therapist, our therapist, a close friend of ours, and our post-adoptive service provider—sitting on our side of the conference room table. We hardly had to say anything during the meeting. The mere presence of these people spoke louder than any of our words could. The teachers and administrators could see how real our son's special need was.

Your attitude in your child's IEP meeting will have long-lasting consequences. You are working hard to receive the services your child needs to succeed, but you are also forming lifelong partnerships with teachers, guidance counselors, and principals.

It's been several years since we've had children at that elementary school, but every time we see one of our son's principals or teachers, the conversation is rich and the spirit is cordial. We walked away from our time at that school loving our experience and loving each staff member.

14

A Girl Named Renee

The Transforming Power of
Love and Compassion

We believe wholeheartedly in the words of Jeremiah 1:5 because we've seen them come to life. On more than one occasion. I shared Tricia's story with you, and now I want to share another story that shows how true the words of this Old Testament prophet are. As I share these powerful stories, I trust you will begin to view your difficult circumstance in a new light. Your situation with the child you are tirelessly trying to parent is filled with hope.

As we have seen, you can experience healing when you find out that you're not alone on the foster and adoptive journey, that others have the same wounds you do—and more. But you can also experience healing when you hear the hope-filled stories that are happening all around us every day.

These are story lines you won't see broadcast on the evening news or the *Today* show. For some reason, we often hear only the dark and awful stories about foster care and adoption. How I wish it weren't the case, but it is. Let's take a few minutes to let a different story fill us with hope.

Renee lived with us through foster care when she was 17 years old. We almost didn't take her into our care, but one of our daughters put the pressure on us big-time. For some reason that is still unknown to us, we caved and emailed the case manager. Within minutes, she replied that she'd be right over with the girl. That should have been our first clue this was not going to be smooth sailing.

Very much like Tricia, Renee pushed as many buttons as she could. She was smart and funny but very wayward. She could look right at you and hear everything you were telling her but refuse to acknowledge you or comply with anything you told her to do. To this day, we still laugh about some of the funny things she said to us. But we also cringe at some of the choices she made.

One of the first nights she lived with us, she came home reeking of marijuana. Her eyes were bloodshot, and she was really, really happy. We knew she was high. But when our second-oldest daughter walked in and said she could smell weed, Renee proceeded to tell us she must have been following a car whose occupants were smoking it and the smoke was blowing back into her car.

I looked at her and said, "Girl, I was born at night, but it wasn't last night." Besides, it was the middle of February in Indiana. If you know anything about the Midwest, it's freezing during that time of year. You'd have to be out of your mind (or actually smoking weed) to have your windows rolled down in the middle of February.

We had so many stories like this with Renee. After she aged out of the foster care system, she asked us if she could continue to live with us until she got on her own feet. We told her she could absolutely live with us. It would be our pleasure. But we had a few simple house rules. The first was that she could not come home drunk or high. She agreed. The second was that she had to participate in our family gatherings (meals and birthdays and such). She agreed to that too. Third, we told her that since we were a pastor's family, it was a value in our family for all of us to go to church. She didn't have to agree with everything she heard, but she had to attend. She hesitantly agreed.

The following Sunday, we were all waiting in the car for Renee to come down and leave with us for church. She had gotten in the shower minutes before our departure. Kristin decided to march back in and demand that she come down. Renee screamed at Kristin from the bathroom that she was not going with us. Kristin reminded her of the agreement, but Renee screamed back that she wasn't going. So my wife, being the brilliant person she is, went down to the basement and turned the hot water off. Renee bolted out of the shower. Standing in our upstairs hallway as naked as the day she was born, she screamed at my wife and called her every name in the book.

Later that afternoon, she disappeared and never returned again. If you had asked me back then what I thought would happen to her, I would have told you matter-of-factly that Renee would end up homeless, in jail, or dead in a matter of months. Everything we saw from her pointed toward one of those outcomes.

Before she left our home we offered to help her get on her feet by paying a $300 deposit on an apartment in our area. We were happy to give her the money. A few days later we noticed she posted a picture on Facebook of a new butterfly tattoo she had across her lower back. A friend commented and asked how much the tattoo was. Renee responded, "Only $300!"

That was money we had given her for a new apartment. But we couldn't expect anything else from a girl who had been through some major trauma, even if she was manipulative, sneaky, and basically a thief.

When she left our home, never to return, we thought the worst would eventually happen to her. We didn't see much hope. But that's where our human minds can only go so far in our thought process and viewpoint. God is limitless in His understanding and His plan. Just when I begin to think that something is a lost cause or there's no way anything good can come from a certain dark situation, He shows me how much I don't know and can't see. This is certainly the case with our journey as foster and adoptive parents. We've faced many dark moments that seemed like dead ends.

> When I begin to think that something is a lost cause, He shows me how much I don't know and can't see.

- Just before we adopted two of the children who had come to us through foster care, they were almost taken to Virginia with a birth family member they had never met—*hopeless!*

- Before our daughter was married or had a solid job, she found out she was pregnant—*bleak!*

- One of our sons made four trips to residential treatment centers—*no future!*

- One of our kids became so depressed, she wanted to end it all at just 11 years old—*heartbreaking!*

It makes you wonder...is this worth it?

Our Limited View

We wonder this because we can't see but a few feet in front of us on most occasions. We're clouded by our present circumstances.

At times it feels like we're driving through dense fog and the head-lights only allow us to see a few feet in front of us. And you know what? It makes complete sense. This is real life. Make no mistake about that. What you're going through with your children is real, heartbreaking stuff. Even though the sun is shining and there is hope, it doesn't erase your present circumstance. It doesn't change what your child is going through. It doesn't change the trauma he's suffered. It doesn't change the fact that he or she is crying out. It's an act of survival.

We know because we face that reality. We're right there in that trench with you. We've had many kids come in and out of our home just like Renee. Because they came from such difficult circumstances, we often felt as if there was no way we could influence them or help them live a different story.

We tend to react to these challenges by compartmentalizing our lives. We zoom in so closely to what we're facing with our children that we leave no room to see the bigger picture around us. The outlook is so bleak, we can't imagine a better reality. These struggles become so much a part of our lives that we are gradually convinced this is as good as it gets. We've zoomed in on our present picture so closely that it's become blurry, out of focus, and pixelated. If only we could see the bigger picture around us. If only our eyesight didn't become blurry after a few feet.

Our daughter (who was 19 years old at the time) and I once had a conversation that got me thinking about our fixation on our current reality. She was sharing some struggles she was having in a rela-tionship, and that led me to say, "We don't realize when we're young that life is so much bigger than our present situation. We focus all our attention and emotion on one pixel of the bigger picture, not

> Struggles become so much a part of our lives that we are gradually convinced this is as good as it gets.

realizing that this is just one pixel. Little by little, as time goes by and we grow older, the rest of the picture comes into view."

How often do we miss the bigger picture of our lives because of our circumstances in the present moment? How often do we find ourselves focusing all our attention and energy on one or two pixels, failing to see the bigger picture around us? How often do our children do this, perhaps because they see their parents doing the same thing?

It's pretty common for our children to focus their attention on one tiny pixel because their emotional makeup and ability to reason are still in development. Their default is to fixate on one problem or issue as if it were the end of their life! How often have you heard that statement screamed in your household? As we raise our children to become productive adults, one of our biggest tasks is to guide them through the seasons of life and help them bring the bigger picture into focus as they grow and mature.

Now, please understand—I'm not discounting major problems or serious personal issues. I realize that many families deal with major trauma or heartbreak. Those moments are crushing blows to the human spirit. My heart breaks for those who have lost loved ones, had a spouse walk out on them, or grieved over a child battling addiction. We live in a fallen world that can appear to be filled with more dark than light. Sometimes our sorrows can encompass more of the picture than just a pixel.

> If we were to take a deep breath, take a step back, and gain some healthy perspective, we'd begin to see these moments in a new light.

What I'm suggesting is that we change our perspective. I believe that in many situations (not all, but many), if we were to take a deep breath, take a step back, and gain some healthy perspective, we'd begin to see these moments in a new light. We thought this situation was the end of the world, or a crisis, or the best that life was going to get, but now we see it as a few pixels of the bigger, brighter picture of our lives. We must teach our children to do this as well as do it ourselves.

I recently came across a clip from the 1986 movie *Ferris Bueller's Day Off.* In this scene, Ferris, his girlfriend Sloan, and his friend Cameron are at an art museum. Cameron is standing before the giant painting *A Sunday Afternoon on the Island of La Grande Jatte*, which is made up entirely of tiny dots (a technique known as pointillism). As Cameron focuses intently on the face of a little girl in the painting, he becomes so focused on the individual dots that make up the image, he loses sight of the girl altogether as well as the portrait as a whole—a beautiful and peaceful portrayal of a time of joy and love. He becomes tense, probably because this is the way he sees his own life too.

The foster and adoptive journey can be like this. Kristin and I know this firsthand, but we've also received hundreds of emails, Facebook comments, and blog comments from readers over the years sharing their own hopeless situations. Some of them write enough to fill a short book.

One mother shared her heartbreak over her daughter, whom she adopted from Haiti, who not only rejects her but acts out physically on her. This single mom is doing the best she can, and she feels as if her life counts for nothing because of her daughter's behavior. I could feel the agony and hopelessness drip from the words in her email to us. It broke our hearts. Reading stories like these, we can understand how a person can get into the habit of zooming in on one pixel of the bigger picture. We've all been there.

But God is limitless in His understanding and His plan. And He's unlimited in what He can see.

Those Who Hope

One of my all-time favorite passages in the Bible is Isaiah 40:28-31.

> Have you never heard?
> > Have you never understood?
> The Lord is the everlasting God,
> > the Creator of all the earth.
> He never grows weak or weary.
> > No one can measure the depths of his understanding.
> He gives power to the weak
> > and strength to the powerless.
> Even youths will become weak and tired,
> > and young men will fall in exhaustion.
> But those who trust in the Lord will find new strength.
> > They will soar high on wings like eagles.
> > They will run and not grow weary.
> > They will walk and not faint (NLT).

He never grows weak or weary (even though we do!). You can't measure the depths of His understanding. He gives us strength when we've run out. If we trust in Him, we will find strength, we won't grow weary, and we won't grow faint.

Isaiah isn't saying we will never face exhaustion or weakness. Rather, as we trust in the Lord on our journey, we will find His strength. We're going to have moments on this journey of sheer exhaustion and defeat, but if we continue to place our hope and trust in our heavenly Father, we'll be rewarded with strength. And by His help we can see the bigger picture of this journey. By placing our trust in the one person

> By placing our trust in the one person who never leaves us or forsakes us, we find the strength to get up and keep going, day after day.

who never leaves us or forsakes us, we find the strength to get up and keep going, day after day.

Notice the verses that precede verse 28:

> God sits above the circle of the earth.
>> The people below seem like grasshoppers to him!
> He spreads out the heavens like a curtain
>> and makes his tent from them.
> He judges the great people of the world
>> and brings them all to nothing.
> They hardly get started, barely taking root,
>> when he blows on them and they wither.
> The wind carries them off like chaff.
> "To whom will you compare me?
>> Who is my equal?" asks the Holy One.
> Look up into the heavens.
>> Who created all the stars?
> He brings them out like an army, one after another,
>> calling each by its name.
> Because of his great power and incomparable strength,
>> not a single one is missing (verses 22-26 NLT).

To whom will you compare Me? Who is My equal? Who created all the stars? These are some of the same questions God asked Job when Job questioned why his life was in shambles. Remember, instead of answers or explanations, God simply offered an invitation. It was an invitation to trust Him through the darkness of Job's situation.

> No life is a hopeless case. No one is without purpose.

When your journey turns out not to be what you expected, trust God. When you're in the thick of parenting a child with extreme special needs and it's just about taking the life out of you, trust Him. When everything is falling apart and the foster care system is jerking you around, trust in His unfailing love. Trust Him through the darkest night. Trust Him, for He is a good Father who loves His kids more than anything. And most of all, trust that He has a great plan for each of your children. No life is a hopeless case. No one is without purpose.

You Have No Idea

I say this with confidence because over the past decade, we've come to realize that when we least expect it, God shows up and brings into focus a beautiful story line we never knew was possible. This has really characterized our journey. Trust me, we're sort of career doubters, and our time as foster and adoptive parents has brought this to the surface more than anything. I would love to tell you that in the darkest moments of our journey, I lifted my hands to the heavens, knelt down to pray, and recited the words of Isaiah 40...but that's not close to my normal response. I fear. I worry. I forget God's promises. I forget that He is with me. I forget what I just told you—that everyone has purpose and a future.

> I have no idea what kind of story God is writing in our lives.

In my (rare) moments of rational thinking, I am reminded that I have no idea what kind of story God is writing in our lives. I have no idea what kind of story He is telling the world through our family and our journey. My hopelessness gives way to this truth. It's a truth that played out in Tricia's life. Even when she was pushing Ruth and Rich away, God was at work in the background of her life. Years later, the plan unfolded.

I'm sure Ruth and Rich both went through seasons of doubt. I'm sure they had those weak, human moments when they looked at Tricia's choices and their present circumstances, concluding that there was no hope. But they continued to trust their heavenly Father, even when the situation was taking the life out of them. And God eventually revealed a story line more beautiful than anything Ruth, Rich, or Tricia could have imagined.

Sometimes the revelation of that story line may be years away. Perhaps you may not even see the transformation or the fulfillment of God's plan in your lifetime.

We lost touch with Renee and didn't hear from her for more than seven years. But a few months ago, Kristin received a Facebook message from Renee. This is what it said.

> Hello, Mike and Kristin,
>
> It's been a very long time, and this message is long over-due, but better late than never, I guess. I owe you both a huge apology, and I don't really know where to start. I hope that this could be the beginnings of an apology anyway. I would just like to say how grateful I am for everything that you guys did for me. I'm forever thankful for your kindness, love, and patience during my time of need while in foster care. I am greatly ashamed of my behavior towards you two and your family, and I apologize for my poor attitude. I consider myself very fortunate to have had so many beautiful and amazing people like you in my life. I feel badly that I haven't always treated them the way they deserved to be treated or returned the love that people expressed towards me. I believe that I've become and am still becoming a better person. I apologize for not being a decent human being toward you and Mike. I hope that you have a wonder-ful day, and thank you for taking the time to read this.

Neither one of us can read her words without choking up. Even though she pushed us to the edge and gave us a run for our money seven years ago, we loved her when she was in our care, and we still do today. We felt hopeless the day she left and in the years after because we forgot one thing. Our Father in heaven is the Author and Creator of all good things, including redemption and grace. When Renee left our home, we thought she was destined for crime, homelessness, or worse. But God had other plans. In the middle of the wreckage, He was writing a story that would not unfold for seven years.

That's why I say emphatically—there is hope for any situation, regardless of how dark and desperate it may be. Grace makes all things possible. Redemption is available to all—no one is out of the reach of God's mercy. It was true for Job, it was true for Tricia and Renee, and I believe it's true for each of our children.

Four Ways to Take Better Care of Yourself

Yawning, yawning, and more yawning. If that describes you, we want you to know you're not alone! There's a way to find rest, and it's not as difficult as you might think.

1. *Stop.* Hit pause on what you're currently doing, because it's probably not working and may have made things a bit worse for you and your journey.

2. *Call for help.* Make a list of five people you can call or text immediately and schedule a time to get coffee together and talk about what's going on with you.

3. *Create a new plan* that helps you reset and recalibrate your parenting and your life.

4. *Take a time-out.* Intentionally carve out time for

you this week. It doesn't have to be a long amount of time, just bite-size. Perhaps a half hour to read in quiet or take a walk in the park. You must be intentional about this.

5. *Move forward* in a new and healthy direction.

We understand the uphill battle of parenting. There is hope for the journey. We've found it, and we want you to find it too.

Hope Has Arrived

God's Beautiful Story in You

The story of Job's life begins with devastation but has a beautiful ending. It would actually make a really good movie. Everything comes back to him—double. You can picture the credits rolling and everyone in the theater applauding as he rides off into the sunset.

> The Lord blessed Job in the second half of his life even more than in the beginning. For now he had 14,000 sheep, 6,000 camels, 1,000 teams of oxen, and 1,000 female donkeys. He also gave Job seven more sons and three more daughters. He named his first daughter Jemimah, the second Keziah, and the third Keren-happuch. In all the land no women were as lovely as the daughters of Job. And their father put them into his will along with their brothers.
>
> Job lived 140 years after that, living to see four generations

of his children and grandchildren. Then he died, an old man who had lived a long, full life (Job 42:12-17 NLT).

God even spared Job's three friends. They entered his story as perfect examples of the people you want around you when your life is in peril. But soon, they become total jerks and not the kind of friends you want preaching at you when your entire life is reduced to a pile of rubble. Still, God accepted Job's prayer on their behalf.

So I guess you could say the story of Job is a bit of a contradiction to the real life we are living day in and day out. How often have we hoped and prayed and trusted that God would bring us through the darkness, only to find matters grow worse? How often have we told God that we trust Him to change the behavior of our children or give us a new perspective on their disorder, only to remain stuck in the rut we were the day or week before?

In the end, Job wins...everything. He gets everything back. He prayed, and voilà...it all came to pass. That's just too good to be true in every case, and it bears little resemblance to our journey. Our situation is probably not going to work out the way Job's did. That's just a reality.

So then, why do I share his story? Where is the hope for us?

The hope is in Jesus. Actually, it's in something He said in John 16.

> But the time is coming—indeed it's here now—when you will be scattered, each one going his own way, leaving me alone. Yet I am not alone because the Father is with me. I have told you all this so that you may have peace in me. Here on earth you will have many trials and sorrows. But take heart, because I have overcome the world (verses 32-33 NLT).

As Jesus was nearing the time of His death, burial, and resurrection, He said a lot of crazy stuff like this to His disciples. It must have left them scratching their heads. Imagine being one of them. For three years you witness some really, really cool stuff from your front-row seat. Tons of people are showing up every time Jesus speaks. Mind-blowing miracles are happening, and everyone is amazed. People who couldn't walk start dancing around. Outcasts become the life of the party.

But then Jesus stops you and says, "Hey, just so you know, life is going to get really hard, I'm going to die soon, and then I'm not going to be around anymore. But trust Me, I'm the boss over all of this!"

Doesn't sound like much fun anymore, does it?

What Jesus was telling His disciples was true though. Life is not getting any easier. This is a journey, not a sprint or even a marathon, and the journey will just about take the life out of you. Why?

Well, because life on earth is hard. Jesus's words were not, "Here on earth you *may* have some painful moments...things *may* get tough...you *could* face death." His words were more like this: "You *will* have trouble...you *will* encounter hardships...you *will* face trials...you *will* be stretched to your limit...life *will* turn out to be different from what you expected...you *will* be in a total battle with your kids at times...you *will* want to quit."

So you've probably wondered, "Where is the hope? Is there any on this journey? Is there any for my family? Is there any for my child? Is there any for me?"

Hope Arriving

As I bring this book to a close, it's Christmastime. All the malls are decked out with colorful lights, ribbons around the trees, frosted window displays, and painted snowflakes up and down the sidewalks. Coffee shops have exchanged their regular to-go cups with red-and-green holiday cups. Radio stations have begun to play Christmas music on loop. Up and down our street, folks have strewn lights on bushes, wrapped them around light poles, and lined them along the gutters of their homes.

There's no doubt it's Christmas.

I'm caught up in the rush of everything, just as I am most years. We just made it through Thanksgiving, and we're counting down the days until Christmas morning. There's shopping to take care of, plans to be made, and Christmas cards to mail. I wonder if we'll be able to fit it all in this year. When you're a foster or adoptive parent and some of your children have sensory processing issues, high anxiety, or an intolerance to high activity, the holidays take on a new form. We have to be conscious of routines and schedules, even when our kids are out of school on break.

In all this rush, however, it's easy to lose sight of what Christmas really is about. I know, every year we hear a similar spiel—Christmas has lost its meaning; it's not about presents or Santa or coffee-shop holiday cup designs or finding the best sale in the mall; it's about Jesus...We've heard it all before.

> When Jesus entered the scene, hope arrived. But it didn't happen the way we usually portray it during this time of the year.

But Christmas really *is* about Jesus. It's about this moment in human history when time was divided. When the darkness was pierced by emerging light. It's the moment when, after nearly 400 years of silence, a voice spoke through the darkness. A Savior was born, and the redemption of the entire world rested on Him. The lost would finally be found, the outcast would finally be accepted, the hurting would finally find healing, the broken would finally be put back together, the sinner would finally be free.

When Jesus entered the scene, hope arrived. But it didn't happen the way we usually portray it during this time of the year.

In a few weeks, we'll join together with others in our church on Christmas Eve and sing songs like "Joy to the World," "The First Noel," and my favorite, "Silent Night." This is usually accompanied by the lighting of candles around the church.

A few years back I worked at a church that had a worship center with two floors of seating on all sides of the stage. Every Christmas Eve, when we lit the candles and sang, the sight was overwhelming. The beautiful melody of a classic Christmas hymn, the soft glow of candlelight, the white Christmas lights strewn throughout the sanctuary...it was completely peaceful and beautiful.

But that's not the way the first Christmas actually went down. When Jesus entered the world, the bloodiest, deadliest, most violent spiritual battle broke out in the heavens. In Revelation 12:1-17, the apostle John records it all.

> When Jesus entered the world, the bloodiest, deadliest, most violent spiritual battle broke out in the heavens.

Then I witnessed in heaven an event of great significance. I saw a woman clothed with the sun, with the moon beneath her feet, and a crown of twelve stars on her head. She was pregnant, and she cried out because of her labor pains and the agony of giving birth.

Then I witnessed in heaven another significant event. I saw a large red dragon with seven heads and ten horns, with seven crowns on his heads. His tail swept away one-third of the stars in the sky, and he threw them to the earth. He stood in front of the woman as she was about to give birth, ready to devour her baby as soon as it was born.

She gave birth to a son who was to rule all nations with an iron rod. And her child was snatched away from the dragon and was caught up to God and to his throne. And the woman fled into the wilderness, where God had prepared a place to care for her for 1,260 days.

Then there was war in heaven. Michael and his angels fought against the dragon and his angels. And the dragon lost the battle, and he and his angels were forced out of heaven. This great dragon—the ancient serpent called the devil, or Satan, the one deceiving the whole world—was thrown down to the earth with all his angels.

Then I heard a loud voice shouting across the heavens,

> "It has come at last—
> salvation and power
> and the Kingdom of our God,
> and the authority of his Christ.
> For the accuser of our brothers and sisters
> has been thrown down to earth—
> the one who accuses them
> before our God day and night.
> And they have defeated him by the blood of the Lamb
> and by their testimony.
> And they did not love their lives so much
> that they were afraid to die.
> Therefore, rejoice, O heavens!
> And you who live in the heavens, rejoice!
> But terror will come on the earth and the sea,
> for the devil has come down to you in great anger,
> knowing that he has little time."

When the dragon realized that he had been thrown down to the earth, he pursued the woman who had given birth to the male child. But she was given two wings like those of a great eagle so she could fly to the place prepared for her in the wilderness. There she would be cared for and protected from the dragon for a time, times, and half a time.

Then the dragon tried to drown the woman with a flood of water that flowed from his mouth. But the earth helped her by opening its mouth and swallowing the river that gushed out from the mouth of the dragon. And the dragon was angry at the woman and declared war against the rest of her children—all who keep God's commandments and maintain their testimony for Jesus (NLT).

This sounds to me like the script for a slasher film or a psychological thriller. One of those films is actually called *Silent Night, Deadly Night*. The film had terrible acting and a weak plotline, but it did have one thing right—the title. The night Jesus was born *was* a deadly night. All hell broke loose...literally. The angels waged war and fought a violent battle against the darkness. Satan's rule over mankind was coming to an end, and he and his demons would not go quietly.

> Jesus takes on hell for you and your children.

Not exactly the type of thing we sing about on Christmas Eve as we light candles, is it? But we need to pay attention to this passage in Revelation. It depicts a battle waged on our behalf. Light won over darkness, and that brings hope to you and me and our children. It brings freedom from the bondage of this world. Our children are often stuck in the rut of their past trauma, and Satan may use that as a tool against them and against us. But remember this: Jesus takes on hell for you and your children.

It's a battle that began when heaven opened and the Son of God descended, wrapped Himself in skin, and became man among us.

The hope that we have is found in no one else but Jesus, the lover of our souls, the healer of our greatest wounds. He gives you and me—parents on this wearisome road—the strength we need to overcome any trial in His name. He also gives our children hope.

Yes, this journey is hard. No, it's not what we thought it would be. Yes, it will almost always be an uphill climb. No, we may never escape the wreckage. Yes, we may always be hands-on in parenting our children. No, there may never be a day when we experience rest fully. Yes, Jesus willingly steps into the wreckage of our lives and this journey, and He holds us together.

I confess that this journey is not what I thought it would be. I've spent more days tired than I have rested. I've been to the darkest places in both thought and action since becoming a parent nearly 15 years ago.

Just this week I visited our son at his school for lunch and felt this way. As I watched him interact with his peers around the lunch table, he snapped at his mother and me (even though we took time out of our day to be with him), and I fielded his disrespectful comments. I thought, "There's no hope. He's always going to be this way. Nothing is ever going to change. Why am I even pretending it is?" But the truth is, God is bigger than our son's 13-year-old behavior. And He has promised that all of us have a hope and a future—me, you, and certainly our son.

Yes, I do lose hope at times. And yes, I do question my purpose. But then I remember that I'm called to do this. And that calling does not depend on my present circumstances. And the love I have for my kids is deeper than the deepest ocean. I couldn't have written a more beautiful, hope-filled story than the one Jesus is writing through us!

Today we kissed our babies on their foreheads and watched them trot off to the bus, and then we grabbed our suitcases and rushed out the door to head to the airport. We're traveling to the same conference I told you about in the introduction. For the next few days, we are going to speak hope into the lives of weary and worn-out foster and adoptive parents.

We're going to tell them about the God who sees them in their deepest anguish and how He holds them together through some of the biggest storms in life. We'll remind them with full hearts that foster care and adoption are worth it because they are quietly but powerfully changing the lives of the children in their care. It doesn't always feel like it, but they are.

We're going to tell them all of this because despite the difficulties of our journey over the past 15 years, we've found an unshakable hope. We've discovered light in the middle of darkness. We've realized how worthy and good the foster and adoptive journeys are. We look back on our story and marvel at it. We couldn't have written a better one ourselves, regardless of how hard we tried. It's only the work of an amazing heavenly Father who promises to never let go of us and to walk with us always.

About the Author

Mike Berry is an author, blogger, speaker, adoptive father, and former foster parent. He and his wife, Kristin, are cocreators of the award-winning blog *confessionsofanadoptiveparent.com*, which has more than 100,000 followers monthly and was named number 3 in the Top 100 Foster Blogs on the Planet in 2017 by Feedspot. It was also named one of the Top Adoptive Mom Blogs in 2016. Mike travels extensively throughout the United States every year with a passion to reach overwhelmed foster and adoptive parents with a message of hope and camaraderie. He is the author of several books, including *The Adoptive Parent Toolbox* and *The Weary Parent's Guide to Escaping Exhaustion*. Mike is also a featured writer on Disney's *babble.com* and on *The Good Men Project*. His work has also appeared on *Yahoo Parent, Your Tango, Huffington Post, MichaelHyatt .com* and *Goinswriter.com*. Mike and Kristin have been married 18 years and have eight children, all of whom are adopted. They reside in the suburbs of Indianapolis, Indiana.

To learn more about Harvest House books and
to read sample chapters, visit our website:

www.harvesthousepublishers.com

HARVEST HOUSE PUBLISHERS
EUGENE, OREGON